THE IMPOSSIBLE QUESTION

J. KRISHNAMURTI

THE IMPOSSIBLE QUESTION

'We are always putting the question of what is possible. If you put an impossible question, your mind then has to find the answer in terms of the impossible — not of what is possible.'

(page 147).

HARPER & ROW, PUBLISHERS
New York, Evanston, San Francisco, London

FIRST UNITED STATES EDITION

STANDARD BOOK NUMBER: 06-064838-x

LIBRARY OF CONGRESS CATALOG CARD NUMBER: 72-78073

CONTENTS

DIALOGUE 4

To see the whole network of fears and escapes. The struggle with attachment is a movement only in fragmentation. Can one arrive at completeness, enlightenment, through fragmentation? How does fragmentation arise? Thought and the category of time. Seeing thought divides and yet is a necessary function, what will you do about it? The function of the mind that is free of the known. To put the impossible question.

DIALOGUE 5

The conscious and the unconscious; what are the frontiers of consciousness? Is this division real, or part of fragmentation? Who 'wants to know' about the unconscious? Neurosis as an exaggeration of fragmentation. The need to see the futility of identification with the fragment; a fragment as 'the observer'. 'Becoming' and 'being something' is the consciousness in which we live: a way of resistance. The difference between seeing this as an observation, and seeing that this is the 'me'. Dreams. Is one in a position to ask the next question: 'What is beyond consciousness'?

DIALOGUE 6

Any action out of fragmentary consciousness produces confusion. Does the content control the structure of consciousness, or is it free of its content? Can consciousness empty itself of its content? The frog in the muddy pool of consciousness trying to get out. The monkey in the space limited by the centre: self-centred activity. What is space without a centre? 'Enlightenment ... is that quality of mind in which the monkey never operates". Attention. The problem of attention and the interruptions of the monkey. With the apogee of attention, what happens to the whole structure of the human being?

Recapitulation. The mind needs order to function properly; thought mistakes security for order. The restless monkey cannot find security. The difference between stability of mind and security. The search for security only brings fragmentation. The mind that is empty of the search for security. 'No such thing as security'. To understand oneself is to understand the movement of thought. The highly attentive mind has no fragmentation of energy. Non-verbal communication. To come upon the state which is vast and timeless, in which 'the concept of death and living has quite a different meaning'.

Page 177

PART I

TALKS AND QUESTIONS

Chapter 1. THE ACT OF LOOKING

*'If you are really serious, then when you look the
old momentum comes to an end.'*

In a world that is so utterly confused and violent, where there
is every form of revolt and a thousand explanations for these
revolts, it is hoped that there will be social reformation, different
realities and greater freedom for man. In every country, in every
clime, under the banner of peace, there is violence; in the name
of truth there is exploitation, misery; there are the starving
millions; there is suppression under great tyrannies, there is
much social injustice. There is war, conscription and the evasion
of conscription. There is really great confusion and terrible
violence; hatred is justified; escapism in every form is accepted
as the norm of life. When one is aware of all this, one is confused, uncertain as to what to do, what to think, what part to
play. What is one to do? Join the activists or escape into some
kind of inward isolation? Go back to the old religious ideas?
Start a new sect, or carry on with one's own prejudices and
inclinations? Seeing all this, one naturally wants to know for
oneself what to do, what to think, how to live a different kind
of life.

If during these talks and discussions we can find a light in
ourselves, a way of living in which there is no violence whatsoever, a way of life which is utterly religious and therefore without fear, a life that is inwardly stable, which cannot be touched
by outward events, then I think they will be eminently worth-
while. Can we give complete and sensitive attention to what we
are going to discuss? We are working together to find out how
to live in peace. It is not that the speaker tells you what to do,

what to think — he has no authority, no 'philosophy'.

There is the difficulty that one's brain functions in old habits, like a gramophone record playing the same tune over and over again. While the noise of that tune, of that habit is going on, one is not capable of listening to anything new. The brain has been conditioned to think in a certain way, to respond according to our culture, tradition and education; that same brain tries to listen to something new and is not capable of it. That is where our difficulty is going to lie. A talk recorded on a tape can be wiped out and begun again; unfortunately the recording on the tape of the brain has been impressed on it for so long that it is very difficult to wipe it out and begin again. We repeat the same pattern, the same ideas and physical habits, over and over again, so we never catch anything fresh.

I assure you one can put aside the old tape, the old way of thinking, feeling, reacting, the innumerable habits that one has. One can do it if one really gives attention. If the thing one is listening to is deadly serious, tremendously important, then one is bound to listen so that the very act of listening will wipe out the old. Do try it — or rather do it. You are deeply interested, otherwise you would not be here. Do listen with full attention, so that in the very act of listening the old memories, the old habits, the accumulated tradition, will all be wiped away.

One has to be serious when confronted with the chaos in the world, the uncertainty, warfare and destruction, where every value has been thrown away in a society which is completely permissive, sexually and economically. There is no morality, no religion; everything is being thrown away and one has to be utterly, deeply serious; if you have that seriousness in your heart, you will listen. It depends on you, not on the speaker, whether you are sufficiently serious to listen so completely as to find out for yourself a light that can never be put out, a way of living that does not depend on any idea, on any circumstance, a way of life that is always free, new, young, vital.

If you have the quality of mind that wants to find out at any price, then you and the speaker can work together and come upon this strange thing that will solve all our problems — whether they be the problems of the daily monotony of life or problems of the most serious nature.

Now how do we go about it? I feel there is only one way, that is: through negation to come to the positive; through understanding what it is not, to find out what it is. To see what one actually is and go beyond that. Start looking at the world and all the events of the world, at the things that are going on; see if one's relation to that is either with or without separation. One can look at the world's events as though they did not concern one as an individual, yet try to shape them, try to do something about them. In that way, there is a division between oneself and the world. One can look that way with one's experience and knowledge, with one's particular idiosyncrasies, prejudices and so on; but it is looking as one separated from the world. One has to find out how to look so that one sees all the things that are happening, outside or inside oneself, as a unitary process, as a total movement. Either one looks at the world from a particular point of view — taking a stand verbally, ideologically, committed to a particular action and therefore isolated from the rest — or one looks at this whole phenomenon as a living, moving process, a total movement of which one is a part and from which one is not divided. What one is, is the result of culture, religion, education, propaganda, climate, food — one is the world and the world is oneself. Can one see the totality of this — not what one should do about it? Does one have this feeling of the wholeness of mankind? It is not a question of identifying oneself with the world, because one is the world. War is the result of oneself. The violence, the prejudice, the appalling brutality that is going on, is part of oneself.

So it depends on how you look at this phenomenon, both inwardly and outwardly, and also on how serious you are. If you are really serious, then when you look, the old momentum

— the repetition of the old patterns, the old ways of thinking, living and acting — come to an end. Are you serious to find out a way of life in which all this turmoil, this misery and sorrow does not exist? For most of us the difficulty lies in being free of the old habits of thought: 'I am something', 'I want to fulfil myself', 'I want to become', 'I believe in my opinions', 'This is the way', 'I belong to this particular sect'. The moment you take a stand you have separated yourself and have therefore become incapable of looking at the total process.

As long as there is the fragmentation of life, both outwardly and inwardly, there must be confusion and war. Do please see this with your heart. Look at the war that is going on in the Middle East. You know all this; there are volumes written explaining it all. We are caught by the explanations — as though any explanation is ever going to solve anything. It is essential to realise that one must not be caught in explanations, it does not matter who gives them. When you see 'what is' it does not demand an explanation; the man who does not see 'what is' is lost in explanations. Please do see this; understand this so fundamentally that you are not caught by words.

In India it is the custom to take their sacred book, the Gita, and explain everything according to that. Thousands upon thousands listen to the explanations as to how you should live, what you should do, how God is this or that — they listen enchanted and yet carry on with their usual life. Explanations blind you, they prevent you from actually seeing 'what is'.

It is vitally important to find out for yourself how you look at this problem of existence. Do you do so from an explanation, from a particular point of view, or do you look non-fragmentarily? Do find out. Go for a walk by yourself and find out, put your heart into finding out how you look at all these phenomena. Then we can work out the details together; and we will go into the most infinite details to find out, to understand. But before we do that you must be very clear that you are free from fragmentation, that you are no longer an Englishman, an American, a Jew — you follow? — that you are free from your conditioning in a particular religion or culture, which tethers you, according to which you have your experiences, which only lead to further conditioning.

Look at this whole movement of life as one thing; there is great beauty in that and immense possibility; then action is extraordinarily complete and there is freedom. And a mind must be free to find out what reality is, not a reality which is invented or imagined. There must be total freedom in which there is no fragmentation. That can only happen if you are really completely serious — not according to somebody who says 'This is the way to be serious'; throw that all away, do not listen to it. Find out for yourself, it does not matter whether you are old or young.

Would you like to ask questions? Before you ask, see why you are asking and from whom you expect the answer. In asking, are you satisfied merely with the explanation which may be the answer? If one asks a question — and one must enquire always about everything — is one asking it because in that very asking one is beginning to enquire and therefore share, move, experience together, create together?

Questioner: If there is someone, say a madman, loose and killing people, and it is within one's power to stop him by killing him, what should one do?

KRISHNAMURTI: So let us kill all the Presidents, all the rulers, all the tyrants, all the neighbours, and yourself! *(Laughter)* No, no, do not laugh. We are part of all this. We have contributed by our own violence to the state the world is in. We do not see this clearly. We think that by getting rid of a few people, by pushing aside the establishment, we are going to solve the whole problem. Every physical revolution has been based on this, the French, the Communist and so on and they have ended up in bureaucracy or tyranny.

14

So my friends, to bring about a different way of living is to bring it about not for others but for oneself; because the 'other' is oneself, there is no 'we' and 'they', there is only ourselves. If one really sees this, not verbally, not intellectually, but with one's heart, then one will see there can be a total action having a completely different kind of result, so there will be a new social structure, not the throwing out of one establishment and the creating of another.

One must have patience to enquire; young people do not have patience, they want instant results — instant coffee, instant tea, instant meditation — which means that they have never understood the whole process of living. If one understands the totality of living there is an action which is instantaneous, which is quite different from the instant action of impatience. Look, see what is going on in America, the racial riots, the poverty, the ghettos, the utter meaninglessness of education as it is — look at the division in Europe, and how long it takes to bring about a Federated Europe. And look at what is happening in India, Asia, Russia and China. When one looks at all that and the various divisions of religion, there is only one answer, one action, a total action, not a partial or fragmentary action. That total action is not to kill another but to see the divisions that have brought about this destruction of man. When one really seriously and sensitively sees that, there will be quite a different action.

Questioner: For someone who is born in a country where there is complete tyranny so that he is totally suppressed, having no opportunity of doing anything himself — I feel most people here cannot imagine it — he is born in this situation and so were his parents, what has he done to create the chaos in this world?

KRISHNAMURTI: Probably he has not done anything. What has the poor man done who lives in the wilds of India, or in a small village in Africa, or in some happy little valley, not knowing

15

anything that is happening in the rest of the world? In what ways has he contributed to this monstrous structure? Probably he has not done anything — poor fellow, what can he do?

Questioner: What does it mean to be serious? I have the feeling that I am not serious.

KRISHNAMURTI: Let us find out together. What does it mean to be serious — so that you are completely dedicated to something, to some vocation, that you want to go right to the end of it. I am not defining it, do not accept any definition. One wants to find out how to live quite a different kind of life, a life in which there is no violence, in which there is complete inward freedom; one wants to find out and intends giving time, energy, thought, everything, to that. I would call such a person a serious person. He is not easily put off — he may amuse himself, but his course is set. This does not mean that he is dogmatic or obstinate, that he does not adjust. He will listen to others, consider, examine, observe. He may in his seriousness become self-centred; that very self-centredness will prevent him from examining; but, he has got to listen to others, he has got to examine, to question constantly; which means that he has to be highly sensitive. He has to find out how and to whom he listens. So he is all the time listening, pursuing, enquiring; he is discovering and with a sensitive brain, a sensitive mind, a sensitive heart — they are not separate things — he is enquiring with the totality and the sensitivity of all that. Find out if the body is sensitive; be aware of its gestures, its peculiar habits. You cannot be sensitive physically if you over-eat, nor can you become sensitive through starvation or fasting. One has to have regard for what one eats. One has to have a brain that is sensitive; that means a brain that is not functioning in habits, pursuing its own particular little pleasure, sexual or otherwise.

Questioner: You have told us not to listen to explanations.

What is the difference between your talks and explanations?

KRISHNAMURTI: What do you think? Is there any difference or is it just the same verbiage going on?

Questioner: Words are words.

KRISHNAMURTI: We explain, giving the description of the cause and the effect, saying, for example: man has inherited brutality from the animal. Someone points that out; but if in the very pointing out you act, you cease to be violent, is there not a difference? Action is what is demanded; but will action come about through explanations, through words? Or does this total action come about only when you are sensitive enough to observe the whole movement of life, the whole of it? What are we trying to do here? Give explanations of 'why' and the cause of 'why'? Or are we trying to live so that our life is not based on words but on the discovery of what actually is — which is not dependent on words. There is a vast difference between the two — even though I point it out. It is like a man who is hungry; you can explain to him the nature and the taste of food, show him the menu, show him through the window the display of food. But what he wants is actual food; and explanations do not give him that. That is the difference.

16th July 1970

Chapter 2. FREEDOM

'The dependence on any form of subjective imagination, fantasy or knowledge, breeds fear and destroys freedom.'

There are many things we have to talk over, but first, it seems to me, we have to consider very deeply what freedom is. Without understanding freedom, not only outwardly, but specially inwardly, deeply and seriously — not merely intellectually, but actually feeling it — whatever we talk about will have very little meaning.

The other day we were considering the nature of the mind. It is the serious mind that really lives and enjoys life — not the mind that is merely seeking entertainment, some particular gratification or fulfilment. Freedom implies the total abnegation and denial of all inward psychological authority. The younger generation thinks freedom is to spit in the face of the policeman, to do whatever it wants. But the denial of outward authority does not mean complete freedom from all inward, psychological authority. When we understand inward authority, the mind and heart are wholly and completely free; then we will be able to understand the action of freedom outwardly.

Freedom of action outwardly, depends entirely on a mind that is free from inward authority. This requires a great deal of patient enquiry and deliberation. It is a matter of primary importance; if it is understood, then we will approach other things which are involved in life and daily living with quite a different quality of mind.

According to the dictionary the meaning of the word 'authority' is: 'one who starts an original idea', 'the author of something entirely new'. He sets up a pattern, a system based on his

18

ideation; others follow it, finding some gratification in it. Or he starts a religious mode of life which others follow blindly, or intellectually. So patterns, or ways of life, of conduct are set up, politically or psychologically, outwardly and inwardly. The mind, which is generally very lazy and indolent, finds it easy to follow what somebody else has said. The follower accepts 'authority' as a means to achieve what is promised by the particular system of philosophy or ideation; he clings to it, depends on it and thereby confirms the 'authority'. A follower then, is a second-hand human being; and most people are completely second-hand. They may think they have some original ideas with regard to painting, writing and so on, but essentially, because they are conditioned to follow, to imitate, to conform, they have become second-hand, absurd human beings. That is one aspect of the destructive nature of authority.

As a human being, do you follow somebody psychologically? We are not talking of outward obedience, the following of the law — but inwardly, psychologically, do you follow? If you do, then you are essentially second-hand; you may do good works, you may lead a very good life, but it all has very little meaning.

There is also the authority of tradition. Tradition means: 'to carry over from the past to the present' — the religious tradition, the family tradition, or the racial tradition. And there is the tradition of memory. One can see that to follow tradition at certain levels has value; at other levels it has no value at all. Good manners, politeness, consideration born out of the alertness of the mind that is watching, can gradually become tradition; the pattern having been set, the mind repeats it. One opens the door for someone, is punctual for meals, and so on. But it has become tradition and is no longer born out of alertness, sharpness and clearness.

The mind which has cultivated memory, functions from tradition like a computer — repeating things over and over again. It can never receive anything new, it can never listen to anything in a totally different way. Our brains are like tape recorders:

19

certain memories have been cultivated through centuries and we keep on repeating them. Through the noise of that repetition one is unable to listen to something new. So one asks: 'What am I to do?' 'How am I to get rid of the old machinery, the old tape?'. The new can be heard only when the old tape becomes completely silent without any effort, when one is serious to listen, to find out, and can give one's attention.

So there is the authority of another on whom we are dependent, the authority of tradition, and the authority of past experience as memory, as knowledge. There is also the authority of the immediate experience, which is recognized from one's past accumulated knowledge; and being recognized, it is no longer something new. How can a mind, a brain, which is so conditioned by authority, imitation, conformity and adjustment, listen to anything completely new? How can one see the beauty of the day, when the mind and the heart and brain are so clouded by the past as authority. If one can actually perceive the fact that the mind is burdened by the past and conditioned by various forms of authority, that it is not free and therefore incapable of seeing completely, then the past is set aside without effort.

Freedom implies the complete cessation of all inward authority. From that quality of mind comes an outward freedom — something which is entirely different from the reaction of opposing or resisting. What we are saying is really quite simple and it is because of its very simplicity that you will miss it. The mind, the brain, is conditioned through authority through imitation and conformity — that is a fact. The mind that is actually free, has no inward authority whatsoever; it knows what it means to love and to meditate.

In understanding freedom one understands also what discipline is. This may seem rather contradictory because we generally think freedom means freedom from all discipline. What is the quality of mind that is highly disciplined? Freedom cannot exist without discipline; which does not mean that you must first be disciplined and then you will have freedom. Freedom and discipline go together, they are not two separate things. So what does 'discipline' mean? According to the dictionary, the meaning of the word 'discipline' is 'to learn' — not a mind that forces itself into a certain pattern of action according to an ideology or a belief. A mind that is capable of learning is entirely different from a mind which is capable only of conforming. A mind that is learning, that is observing, seeing actually 'what is', is not interpreting 'what is' according to its own desires, its own conditioning, its own particular pleasures.

Discipline does not mean suppression and control, nor is it adjustment to a pattern or an ideology; it means a mind that sees 'what is' and learns from 'what is'. Such a mind has to be extraordinarily alert, aware. In the ordinary sense, 'to discipline oneself' implies that there is an entity that is disciplining itself according to something. There is a dualistic process: I say to myself, 'I must get up early in the morning and not be lazy', or 'I must not be angry'. That involves a dualistic process. There is the one who with his will tries to control what he should do, as opposed to what he actually does. In that state there is conflict.

The discipline laid down by parents, by society, by religious organizations means conformity. And there is revolt against conformity — the parent wanting one to do certain things, and the revolt against that, and so on. It is a life based on obedience and conformity; and there is the opposite of it, denying conformity and to do what one likes. So we are going to find out what the quality of the mind is that does not conform, does not imitate, follow and obey, yet has a quality in itself which is highly disciplined — 'disciplined' in the sense of constantly learning.

Discipline is learning, not conforming. Conformity implies comparing myself with another, measuring myself as to what I am, or think I should be, against the hero, the saint, and so on. Where there is conformity there must be comparison — please see this. Find out whether you can live without comparison, which means, not to conform. We are conditioned from childhood to compare — 'You must by like your brother, or your great-aunt'; 'You must by like the saint', or 'Follow Mao'. We compare in our education, in schools there is the giving of marks and the passing of examinations. We do not know what it means to live without comparison and without competition, therefore non-aggressively, non-competitively, non-violently. Comparing yourself with another is a form of aggression and a form of violence. Violence is not only killing or hitting somebody, it is in this comparative spirit, 'I must be like somebody else', or 'I must perfect myself'. Self-improvement is the very antithesis of freedom and learning. Find out for yourself how to live a life without comparing, and you will see what an extraordinary thing happens. If you really become aware, choicelessly, you will see what it means to live without comparison, never using the words 'I will be'.

We are slaves to the verb 'to be', which implies: 'I will be somebody sometime in the future'. Comparison and conformity go together; they breed nothing but suppression, conflict and endless pain. So it is important to find a way of daily living in which there is no comparison. Do it, and you will see what an extraordinary thing it is; it frees you from so many burdens. The awareness of that brings about a quality of mind that is highly sensitive and therefore disciplined, constantly learning — not what it wants to learn, or what is pleasurable, gratifying to learn, but *learning*. So you become aware of inward conditioning resulting from authority, conformity to a pattern, to tradition, to propaganda, to what other people have said, and of your own accumulated experience and that of the race and the family. All of that has become the authority. Where there is authority, the mind can never be free to discover whatever there is to be discovered — something timeless, entirely new.

A mind that is sensitive is not limited by any set pattern; it is constantly moving, flowing like a river, and in that constant movement there is no suppression, no conformity, no desire to fulfil. It is very important to understand clearly, seriously and deeply, the nature of a mind that is free and therefore truly religious. A mind that is free sees that dependency on something — on people, on friends, on husband or wife, on ideation, authority and so on — breeds fear; *there* is the source of fear. If I depend on you for my comfort, as an escape from my own loneliness and ugliness, from shallowness and pettiness, then that dependence breeds fear. Dependence on any form of subjective imagination, fantasy, or knowledge, breeds fear and destroys freedom.

When you see what it all implies — how there is no freedom when there is dependence inwardly and therefore fear, and how it is only a confused and unclear mind that depends — you say: 'How am I to be free from dependency?' Which is again another cause of conflict. Whereas, if you observe that a mind that depends must be confused, if you know the truth, that a mind that depends inwardly on any authority only creates confusion — if you see that, without asking how to be free of confusion — then you will cease to depend. Then your mind becomes extraordinarily sensitive and therefore capable of learning and it disciplines itself without any form of compulsion or conformity.

Is all this somewhat clear — not verbally but actually? I can imagine, or think that I see very clearly, but that clarity is very short-lived. The real quality of clear perception comes only when there is no dependency, and therefore not that confusion which arises when there is fear. Can you honestly, seriously, bring yourself to find out whether you are free from authority? It needs tremendous enquiry into yourself, great awareness. From that clarity comes a totally different kind of action, an action that is not fragmentary, that is not divided politically or religiously — it is a total action.

Questioner: From what you have said, it seems that an action which at one point can be thought to be a reaction to some outward authority, can be a total action at another point, by another individual.

KRISHNAMURTI: Intellectually, verbally, we can compete with each other, explain each other away, but that does not mean a thing; what to you may be a complete action may appear to me as incomplete action — that is not the point. The point is whether your mind, as that of a human being, acts completely. A human being of the world — you understand? — is not an individual. 'Individual' means indivisible. An individual is one who is undivided in himself, who is non-fragmentary, who is whole, sane, healthy; also 'whole' means holy. When you say 'I am an individual', you are nothing of the kind. Live a life of no authority, of no comparison, and you will find out what an extraordinary thing it is; you have tremendous energy when you are not competing, not comparing and not suppressing; you are really alive, sane, whole and therefore sacred.

Questioner: What you are saying is not very clear to me. What can I do?

KRISHNAMURTI: Either what is said is not very clear in itself or you may not understand English properly, or you are not sustaining attention all the time. It is very difficult to sustain attention for an hour and ten minutes; there are moments when you are not giving complete attention and then you say, 'I have not quite understood what you are talking about'. Find out whether you are sustaining attention, listening, watching, or if you go wandering off, vagabonding. Which is it?

Questioner: Do you think it is possible to learn all the time?

KRISHNAMURTI: When you ask that question of yourself, you have already made it difficult. By putting a question of that kind you are preventing yourself from learning — you see the point? I am not concerned with whether I am going to learn all the time, I'll find out. What I am concerned with is: am I learning? If I am learning, I am not concerned as to whether it is 'all the time' — I don't make a problem of it. The question becomes irrelevant if I am learning.

Questioner: You can learn from anything.

KRISHNAMURTI: That is, if you are aware that you are learning. This is very complex: may I go into it a little?

'Can I learn all the time'? Which factor is important here? 'Learning', or 'all the time'? — obviously it is 'learning'. When I am learning I am not concerned with 'the rest of the time', the time-interval and so on. I am only concerned with what I am learning. Naturally the mind wanders off, it gets tired, it becomes inattentive. Being inattentive, it does all kinds of stupid things. So it is not a question of how to make the inattentive mind attentive. What is important is for the inattentive mind to become aware that it is inattentive. I am aware, watching everything, the movement of the trees, the flow of the water, and I am watching myself — not correcting, not saying this should be or this should not be — just watching. When the mind that is watching gets tired and becomes inattentive, suddenly it becomes aware of this, and tries to force itself to become attentive; so there is a conflict between inattention and attention. I say: do not do that, but become aware that you are inattentive — that is all.

Questioner: Could you describe how you are aware that you are inattentive?

KRISHNAMURTI: I am learning about myself — not according to some psychologist or specialist — I am watching and I see something in myself; but I do not condemn it, I do not judge it, I do not push it aside — I just watch it. I see that I am proud — let us take that as an example. I do not say, 'I must put it aside, how ugly to be proud' — but I just watch it. As I am watching I am learning. Watching means learning what pride involves, how it has come into being. I cannot watch it for more than five or six minutes — if one can, that is a great deal — the next moment I become inattentive. Having been attentive and knowing what inattention is, I struggle to make inattention attentive. Do not do that, but watch inattention, become aware that you are inattentive — that is all. Stop there. Do not say, 'I must spend all my time being attentive', but just watch when you are inattentive. To go any further into this would be really quite complex. There is a quality of mind that is awake and watching all the time, watching though there is nothing to learn. That means a mind that is extraordinarily quiet, extraordinarily silent. What has a silent, clear mind to learn?

Questioner: Could not communicating with words, with ideas, become a habit, a tradition?

KRISHNAMURTI: They become a habit, a tradition, only when they become important as words. There must be verbal communication, which is to share whatever we are looking at together — like fear; that means you and the speaker are both at the same level, at the same time, with the same intensity, observing, co-operating, sharing. That brings about a non-verbal communion which is not habit.

Questioner: How is it possible for a total, whole, sane individual, who is not fragmented but indivisible, to love another? How can a whole human being love a fragmented human being? Further, how can a whole individual love another whole individual?

KRISHNAMURTI: You cannot be whole if you do not know what love is. If you are whole — in the sense we are talking about — then there is no question of loving another. Have you ever watched a flower by the roadside. It exists, it lives in the sun, in the wind, in the beauty of light and colour, it does not say to you: 'Come and smell me, enjoy me, look at me' — it lives and its very action of living is love.

19th July 1970

Chapter 3. ANALYSIS

'Analysis is never complete; the negation of that incomplete action is total action.'

It is really quite important to understand the whole problem of living: from the moment we are born till we die, we are always in conflict. There is always a struggle, not only within ourselves, but outwardly in all our relationships, there is strain and strife; there is constant division, and a sense of the separate individual existence in opposition to the community. In the most intimate relationships, each one is seeking his own pleasure, secretly or openly; each one is pursuing his own ambition and fulfilment, thereby generating frustration. What we call living, is turmoil. In this turmoil we try to be creative. If one is gifted one writes a book or a poem, composes a picture and so on, but all within the pattern of strife, grief and despair; yet this is what is considered creative living. In going to the moon, living under the sea, waging wars, there is this constant bitter strife of man against man. This is our life.

It seems to me that we should go into this matter very seriously, very deeply, and if we can, feel our way into a quality of mind where there is no strife whatsoever, both at the conscious level and also in the layers that lie below the conscious.

Beauty is not the result of conflict. When you see the beauty of a mountain or of swift running water, in that immediate perception there is no sense of striving. In our lives there is not much beauty because of the battle that is going on.

To find a quality of mind that is essentially beautiful and clear, that has never been touched by strife, is of the greatest importance; in the understanding of that — not merely verbally

27

or intellectually, but in actually living it in daily life — we may have some kind of peace within ourselves and in the world. Perhaps this morning we shall be able, hesitantly and with sensitive watchfulness, to understand this battle we live in, and be free of it.

What is the root-cause of this conflict and contradiction? Ask this question of yourself. Do not try to put into words an explanation, but simply enquire non-verbally, if you can, into the basis of this contradiction and division, this strife and conflict. Either you enquire analytically or you perceive immediately the root of it. Analytically, you may unravel bit by bit and come upon the nature, the structure, the cause and effect of this strife within ourselves, between the individual and the State. Or you may perceive the cause of it instantly. In this way we may find out factually the cause of all this conflict and perceive the truth of it instantly.

Let us understand what it means to analyse, to attempt to discover intellectually, verbally, the cause of this conflict. Because once you understand the analytical process — see the truth or the falseness of it — you will be completely free of it for ever; which implies an understanding in which your eyes, your mind, and your heart perceive immediately the truth of the matter. We are used to, conditioned to, the analytical process and the philosophical and psychological approach of the various specialists; it has become a habit. We are conditioned to trying to understand this whole complex process of living analytically, intellectually. This is not to advocate its opposite — emotional sentimentality. But if you understand very clearly the nature and the structure of the analytical process, then you will have quite a different outlook; you will be able to direct the energy which had been given to analysis in a totally different direction.

Analysis implies division. There is the analyser and that which is to be analysed. Whether you analyse yourself, or it is done by a specialist, there is division, therefore there is already the beginning of conflict. We can do tremendous things only when

28

there is great passion, great energy, and it is only this passion that can create a totally different kind of life in ourselves and in the world. That is why it is very important to understand this process of analysis in which the human mind has been caught for centuries.

Of the many fragments into which we are divided, one assumes the authority of the analyser; the thing that is to be analysed is another. That analyser becomes the censor; he, with his accumulated knowledge, evaluates the good and the bad, what is right and what is wrong, what should or should not be suppressed, and so on. Also, the analyser must make every analysis complete, otherwise his evaluation, his conclusion, will be partial. The analyser must examine every thought — everything which he thinks should be analysed, and that will take time. You may spend a whole lifetime analysing — if you have the money and the inclination, or if you can find an analyst with whom you are in love, and all the rest of it. You can spend all your days analysing and at the end of it you are where you were, with still more to be analysed.

We see that in analysis there is the division between the analyser and the analysed, and also that the analyser must analyse accurately, completely, or his conclusions will impede the next analysis. We see that the analytical process takes an infinite time and during that time many other things may happen. So when you see the whole structure of analysis, then that seeing is actually a denial, a negation of it; seeing what is involved in it, there is the negation of that action — which is complete action.

Questioner: What do you mean by action?

KRISHNAMURTI: Action according to an idea, an ideology, one's accumulated experience. Action is always approximating itself to the ideal, to the prototype, so there is a division between action and ideal. Such action is never complete, analysis is never complete; the negation of that incomplete action is total action.

When the mind has seen the futility, the meaninglessness of analysis, with all the problems which are involved, it will never touch it; the mind will never seek to understand 'true' analysis.

The mind that has looked into the process of analysis has become very sharp, alive, sensitive, because it has rejected that which we had considered to be the way and means of understanding.

If you see very clearly for yourself — not forced or compelled by the argument and reasoning of another — the falseness or the truth of analysis, then your mind is free and has the energy to look in another direction. What is the 'other direction'? It is the immediacy of perception that is total action.

As we said, there is division between the analyser and the thing to be analysed, division between the observer and the thing observed: this is the root-cause of conflict. When you observe, you always do so from a centre, from the background of experience and knowledge; the 'me' as the Catholic, the Communist, the 'specialist' and so on, is observing. So there is a division between 'me' and the thing observed. This does not require a great deal of understanding, it is an obvious fact. When you look at a tree, at your husband, or wife, there is this division. It exists between yourself and the community. So there is this observer and the thing observed: in that division there is inevitably contradiction. That contradiction is the root of all strife.

If that is the root-cause of conflict, then the next question is: can you observe without the 'me', the censor, without all the accumulated experiences of misery, conflict, brutality, vanity, pride, despair, which are the 'me'? Can you observe without the past — the past memories, conclusions and hopes, without all the background? That background — as the 'me', the 'observer' — divides you from the observed. Have you ever observed without the background? Do it now, please. Play with it. Look at the outward things objectively; listen to the noise of the river, look at the lines of the mountains, the beauty, the clarity of it all.

That is fairly easy to do without the 'me', as the past, observing. But can you look at yourself inwardly, without the observer? Do, please, look at yourself, your conditioning, your education, your way of thinking, your conclusions, your prejudices, without any kind of condemnation or explanation or justification — just observe. When you so observe there is no 'observer' and therefore no conflict.

That way of living is totally different from the other — it is not the opposite, not a reaction to the other, it is entirely different. And in it there is tremendous freedom and an abundance of energy and passion. It is total observation, complete action. When you have completely seen and understood, your action will always be clear. It is like looking at the total extent of the map, not the detail of where you want to go.

So one finds out for oneself, as a human being, that it is possible to live without any kind of conflict. This implies an enormous revolution in oneself. *That is the only revolution.* Every form of physical, outward revolution — political, economic, social — always ends up in dictatorship, either of the bureaucrats or of the idealist or of some conqueror. Whereas this inward, complete and total revolution, which is the outcome of the understanding of all conflict, which is caused by the division between the observer and the observed, brings about a totally different kind of living.

Now please let us go into it further, if you will, by asking questions about it.

Questioner: How can one divorce oneself from problems, when one lives in a world full of problems?

KRISHNAMURTI: Are you different from the world? You are the world — are you not?

Questioner: I am just a person who lives in the world.

KRISHNAMURTI: 'Just a person who lives in the world' — dis-

31

associated, unrelated to all the events that are taking place in the world?

Questioner: No, I am part of that. But how can I divorce myself from it?

KRISHNAMURTI: You cannot possibly divorce yourself from the world: you are the world. If you live in Christendom, you are conditioned by the culture, by the religion, by the education, by the industrialization, by all the conflicts of its wars. You cannot possibly separate yourself from that world. The monks have tried to withdraw from the world, enclosing themselves in a monastery, but nevertheless, they are the result of the world in which they live; they want to escape from that culture by withdrawing from it, by devoting themselves to what they consider to be the truth, to the ideal of Jesus and so on.

Questioner: How can I look into myself with all the worries that are on my mind, with making money, buying a house, and so on?

KRISHNAMURTI: How do you look at your job? How do you consider it?

Questioner: I consider it as a means to survive in the world.

KRISHNAMURTI: 'I must have a livelihood in order to survive.' The whole structure of society, whether here, or in Russia, is based on survival at any price, doing something which society has set up. How can one survive safely, lastingly, when there is division between ourselves? When you are a European and I am an Asian, when there is division between ourselves, each one competing to be secure, to survive, therefore battling with each other individually and collectively, how can there be survival? A temporary survival?

So the real question is, not that of survival, but whether it is possible to live in this world without division; when there is no division we shall survive, completely, without fear. There have been religious wars; there have been appalling wars between the Catholics and the Protestants — each saying, 'We must survive'. They never said to themselves, 'Look, how absurd this division is, one believing this and the other believing that'; they never saw the absurdity of their conditioning. Can we put the whole energy of our thinking, our feeling, our passion, into finding out whether it is possible to live without this division, so that we shall live fully, in complete security? But you are not interested in all that. You just want to survive. You don't — your survival is in spite of non-survival.

Look Sirs, sovereign governments, each with their own army, have divided the world and are at each other's throats, maintaining prestige and economic survival. Computers, without the politicians, in the hands of good men, can alter the whole structure of this world. But we are not interested in the unity of mankind. Yet, politically, that is the only problem. That can only be solved when there are no politicians, when there are no sovereign governments, when there are no separate religious sects — and you, who are listening to this, you are the people to do it.

Questioner: Does it not need conscious analysis to arrive at that conclusion?

KRISHNAMURTI: Is it a conclusion, resulting from analysis? You just observe this fact. Look at how the world is divided by sovereign governments and religions; you can see it — is that analysis?

Questioner: Don't you think that in order to change all that, we also need an outward revolution?

KRISHNAMURTI: An inward and an outward revolution at the

same time. Not first one and then the other; it must be simultaneous. It must be an instant inward and outward revolution without emphasising one or the other. How can that take place? Only when you see the complete truth, that the inward revolution is the outward revolution. When you see that, then it takes place — and not intellectually, verbally, ideally. But is there in you a complete inward revolution? If there is not and you want outer revolution, then you are going to bring chaos into the world. And there *is* chaos in the world.

Questioner: You speak of Governments, and Churches, and Nationalism; they have what we consider to be the power.

KRISHNAMURTI: The bureaucrats want power and they have it. Don't you want power — over your wife or your husband? In your conclusions as to what you think is right, there is power; every human being wants some kind of power. So don't attack the power that is vested in others, but be free of the demand for power in yourself; then your action will be totally different. We want to attack the outward power, tear that power away from the hands of those who have it and give it to somebody else; we do not say to ourselves, 'Let us be free of all dominance and possession'. If you actually applied your whole mind to be free of every kind of power — which means to function without status — then you would bring about quite a different society.

Questioner: If you are hungry you can't even begin to deal with these questions.

KRISHNAMURTI: If you were really hungry you would not be here! We are not hungry and therefore we have time to listen, time to observe. You may say, we are a small group of people, a drop in the ocean, what can we do? Is that a valid question when we are confronted with this enormously complex problem of the world in which we live? As a human being, a simple

34

individual, what can I do? If you were really confronted with the problem would you put that question? You would just be working — you understand Sir? When you say, 'What can I do?', in that is already a note of despair.

Questioner: A lot of people are hungry, they have to take immediate steps to survive. What does all this mean to them?

KRISHNAMURTI: Nothing. When I am hungry Sir, I want food — and all this has very little meaning. So what is your question?

Questioner: We are a minority, a small group. The vast majority, in India, in Asia, in parts of Europe and America, are really hungry. How can what we are saying here, affect all these people?

KRISHNAMURTI: It depends on you, on what you do, even as the small minority. An enormous revolution in the world is created because a minority in themselves have changed. You are concerned with the misery of the world, the poverty, the degradation, the starvation, and you say, 'What can I do?' Either you thoughtlessly join an outward revolution, try to break it all up and create a new kind of social structure — and in the process of that you will again establish the same misery — or you will consider a total revolution, not partial, not merely physical, in which the inward structure of the psyche will act in an entirely different relationship with society.

Questioner: You speak as though inward revolution happens suddenly — does it really take place that way?

KRISHNAMURTI: Is the inward revolution a matter of time, of gradual inward change? This is a very complex question. We are conditioned to accept that through gradual inward revolution there will be a change. Does it take place step by step, or does it happen instantly when you see the truth of the matter? When you see instant danger there is instant action — is there not? Then your action is not gradual or analytical; when there is danger, there is immediate action. We are pointing out the dangers — the dangers of analysis, the danger of power, of postponement, of division. When you see the real danger of it — not verbally, but actually, physically and psychologically — then there is instant action, the action of an instant revolution. To see these psychological dangers you need a sensitive, alert, watchful mind. If you say, 'How am I to have a watchful, a sensitive mind?' you are again caught in gradualness. But when you see the necessity as when confronted by danger — and society is danger, all the things you are involved in are dangerous — then there is a total action.

21st July, 1970.

Chapter 4. FRAGMENTATION

'A problem only arises when life is seen fragmentarily.
Do see the beauty of that.'

KRISHNAMURTI: When we face our innumerable problems we
are inclined to try to solve each problem by itself. If it is a
sexual problem, we treat it as though it were something totally
unrelated to other problems. Equally with the problem of violence or starvation, which we try to solve politically, economically or socially. I wonder why we try to solve each problem by
itself. The world is ridden with violence; the various powers
that be try to solve each problem as though it were something
apart from the rest of life. We do not consider these problems
as a whole, seeing each problem related to other problems and
not in isolation.

Violence, as one can see in oneself, is part of our animal
inheritance. A great part of us is animal, and without understanding the structure of ourselves as whole human beings,
merely trying to solve violence by itself only leads to further
violence. I think this must be clearly understood by each of us.
There are thousands of problems which appear to be separate,
which we never seem to see as interrelated, but no problem can
be solved in isolation by itself. We have to deal with life as a
continuous movement of problems and crises, great or small.
Let us go into this very carefully, because unless it is clearly
understood when we discuss the questions of fear, love, death,
meditation and reality, we shall not understand how they are
all interrelated. For the beauty of life, the ecstasy, the thing
that is immeasurably vast, is not separate from our daily problems. If you say, 'I am only concerned with meditation and

with truth', you will never find it, but do understand how all problems are interrelated. For instance starvation, which cannot be stopped by itself, for it is a problem involving the national, political, economic, social, religious and psychological divisions between man and man. And we have the problem of personal relationship, the problem of suffering — not only physical but psychological suffering — problems of intense sorrow, not only personal sorrow but the sorrow of the world, its misery and confusion. If we try to find an answer to each particular problem, then we only bring about further division, further conflict. If you are at all serious and mature you must have asked why the mind tries to solve each problem as though it were unrelated to other problems. Why does the human mind, the brain, always divide as 'me' and 'mine', 'we' and 'they', religion and politics and so on? Why is there this constant division with all the effort to solve each problem by itself in isolation?

To answer that question we have to enquire into the function of thought, its meaning, substance and structure; because it may be that thought itself divides, and that the very process of trying to find an answer through thinking, through reasoning, causes separation.

People want a physical revolution in order to bring about a better order, forgetting all the implications of physical revolution, forgetting the whole psychological nature of man. So one has to ask this question. And what is the response? Is it the response of thought, or is it the response of understanding the totality of this vast structure of human life?

We want to find out why this division exists. We went into it the other day, as the 'observer' and the 'observed'. Let us put that aside and approach it differently. Does thought create this division? If we find it does, it is because thought tries to find an answer to a particular problem separated from other problems.

Do not, please, agree with me; it is not a question of agreement, it is a question of seeing for yourself the truth or the falseness of it. Under no circumstances accept what the speaker says at any time. There is no authority, neither you nor the speaker have authority; both of us are investigating, observing, looking, learning.

If thought, by its very nature and structure, divides life into many problems, trying to find an answer through thought will only lead to an isolated answer, therefore we see that it breeds further confusion, further misery. One has to find out for oneself, freely, without any bias, without any conclusion, if thought operates this way. Most of us try to find an answer intellectually or emotionally, or say we do so intuitively. One must be very careful of that word 'intuition'; in that word lies great deception, because one can have intuition dictated by one's own hopes, fears, bitterness, wishes and so on. We try to find an answer intellectually or emotionally, as though the intellect were something separate from emotion and emotion something separate from the physical response. Our education and culture together with all our philosophical concepts are based on this intellectual approach to life; our social structure and our morality are based on this division.

So if thought divides, how does it divide? If you actually observe it in yourself you will see what an extraordinary thing you will discover. You will be a light to yourself, you will be an integrated human being, not looking to somebody else to tell you what to do, what to think and how to think. Thought can be extraordinarily reasonable; it must reason consecutively, logically, objectively, sanely; it must function perfectly, like a computer ticking over without any hindrance, without any conflict. Reasoning is necessary; sanity is part of the reasoning capacity.

Can thought ever be new, fresh? Every human problem — not the mechanical and scientific problem — but every human problem is always new and thought tries to understand it, tries to alter it, tries to translate it, tries to do something about it.

If we deeply felt love for each other — not verbally but

really — then all this division would come to an end. That can only take place when there is no conditioning, when there is no centre as the 'me' and the 'you'. But thought, which is the activity of the brain, of the intellect, cannot possibly love. Thought has to be understood and we ask whether thought can see anything new; or is it that the 'new' thought is always old, so that when it faces a problem of life — which is always new — it cannot see the newness of it because it tries to translate it in terms of its own conditioning.

Thought is necessary, yet we see that thought divides, as the 'me' and 'not me'; it tries to solve the problem of violence in isolation, unrelated to all other problems of existence. Thought is always of the past: if we had not the brain, which like a tape-recorder has accumulated all kinds of information and experience, we would not be able to think or respond. Thought, meeting a new issue, must translate it in its own terms of the past and therefore creates division.

Leave everything aside for the moment and observe your thinking: it is the response of the past. If you had no thought there would be no past, there would be a state of amnesia. Thought inevitably divides life into the past, present and future. As long as there is thought, as the past, life must be divided into time.

If I want to understand the problem of violence completely, totally, so that the mind is altogether free from violence, I can only understand it by understanding the structure of thought. It is thought that breeds violence: 'my' house, 'my' wife, 'my' country, 'my' belief, which is utter nonsense. Who is the ever-lasting 'me' opposed to the rest? What causes it? Is it education, society, the establishment, the church? They are all doing it and I am part of all that. Thought is matter; it is in the very struct-ure, in the very cells of the brain so when the brain operates — whether psychologically, socially, or religiously — it must invariably operate in terms of its past conditioning. We see that thought is essential and must function absolutely logically, objectively, impersonally, and yet we see how thought divides.

I am not pushing you to agree, but do you see that thought must inevitably divide? Look what has happened: thought sees that nationalism has led to all kinds of war and mischief, so it says, 'Let us all be united, form a league of nations'. But thought is still operating, still maintaining the separation — you, as an Italian, keeping your Italian sovereignty and so on. There is talk about brotherhood yet the maintaining of separation, which is hypocrisy. It is characteristic of thought to play double games within itself.

So thought is not the way out — which does not mean kill the mind. What then is it that sees every problem as it arises in its totality? A sexual problem is a total problem, related to culture, to character, to the various issues of life — not a fragment of the problem. What mind is it that sees each problem totally?

Questioner: I have understood, but still there remains a question.

KRISHNAMURTI: When you have understood what thought does, at the highest and at the lowest level, yet when you say there is still another question, who is it that is asking that question? When the brain, the whole nervous system, the mind — which covers all of that — says, 'I have understood the nature of thought', then the next step is: one sees whether this mind can look at the entirety of life with all its vastness and complexity, with its apparently unending sorrow. That is the only question and thought is not putting that question. The mind has observed the whole structure of thought and knows its relative value; can this mind look with an eye that is never spotted by the past?

This is really a very serious question, not just an entertainment. One must give one's energy, passion, one's life to find out; because this is the only way out of this terrible brutality, sorrow, degradation, everything that is corrupt. Can the mind, the brain — which is itself corrupt through time — be quiet, so that it can see life as a whole and therefore without problems? A problem only arises when life is seen fragmentarily. Do see the beauty of that. When you see life as a whole then there is no problem whatsoever. It is only a mind and a heart that is broken up in fragments that creates problems. The centre of the fragment is the 'me'. The 'me' is brought about through thought; *it has no reality by itself.* The 'me' — 'my' house, 'my' disappointment, 'my' desire to become somebody — that 'me' is the product of thought which divides. Can the mind look without the 'me'? Not being able to do this, that very 'me' says: 'I will dedicate myself to Jesus' — 'to Buddha, to this, to that' — you understand? — 'I will become a Communist who will be concerned with the whole of the world'. The 'me' identifying itself with what it considers to be greater, is still the 'me'.

So the question arises: can the mind, the brain, the heart, the whole being, observe without the 'me'. The 'me' is of the past; there is no 'me' in the present. The present is not of time. Can the mind be free of the 'me' to look at the whole vastness of life? It can, completely, utterly, when you have fundamentally, with all your being, understood the nature of thinking. If you have not given your attention, everything you have, to find out what thinking is, you will never be able to find out if it is possible to observe without the 'me'. If you cannot observe without the 'me' the problems will go on — one problem opposing another. And all these problems will come to an end, I assure you, when man lives a different life altogether, when the mind can look at the world as a total movement.

Questioner: At the beginning of the talk you were asking what made us try to solve problems separately. Is not urgency one of the reasons which cause us to try to solve problems separately?

KRISHNAMURTI: If you see danger you act. In that action there is no question of urgency, no impatience — you act. The urgency and the demand for immediate action, takes place only when you see the danger as a danger to the 'me' as thought. When you see the total danger of thought dividing the world, that seeing is the urgency and the action. When you really see starvation, such as there is in India, and see how the starvation has been brought about, the callousness of people, of governments, the inefficiency of the politicians, what do you do? Tackle one area of starvation by itself? Or do you say 'This whole thing is a psychological issue, it is centred in the 'me' which is brought about by thought'? If that starvation in all its forms is completely, totally, understood — not only physical starvation, but the human starvation of having no love — you will find the right action. The very change *is* urgency; it is not that change will come about through urgency.

Questioner: You seem to say that thought has to function, at the same time you say it cannot.

KRISHNAMURTI: Thought must function logically, non-personally and yet thought must be quiet. How can this take place?

Do you actually see, or understand, the nature of thinking — not according to me or to a specialist — do you yourself see how thought works? Look Sir: when you are asked a question on a matter which is utterly familiar to you, your response is immediate, is it not? When you are asked a little more complicated question you take more time. If the brain is asked a question to which it cannot find an answer having searched all its memories and books it says, 'I do not know'. Has it used thought to say 'I do not know'? When you say, 'I do not know', your mind is not seeking, not waiting, not expecting; the mind which says 'I do not know' is entirely different from the mind which operates with knowledge. So can the mind remain completely free of knowledge and yet operate functionally in the field of the known? The two are not divided. When you want to discover something new you have to put the past aside. The new can take place only when there is freedom from the known. That freedom can be constant; which means that the mind lives in complete silence, in nothingness. This nothingness and silence is vast, and out of that, knowledge — technical knowledge — can be used to work things out. Also, out of that silence can be observed the whole of life — without the 'me'.

Questioner: You were saying in the beginning of the talk, that to want to change things from the outside, would lead to the dictatorship of a group or person. Don't you think that we are now living under the dictatorship of money and industry?

KRISHNAMURTI: Of course. Where there is authority there is dictatorship. To bring about a social, a religious or a human change, there must be first understanding of the whole structure of thought as the 'me', which is seeking power — whether it is I, or the other who is seeking power. Can the mind live without seeking power? Answer this, Sir.

Questioner: Is it not natural to seek power?

KRISHNAMURTI: Of course it is so-called natural. So is the dog seeking power over other dogs. But we are supposed to be cultured, educated, intelligent. Apparently after millenia we have not learnt to live without power.

Questioner: I wonder whether the mind can ever put a question about itself to which it does not already know the answer.

KRISHNAMURTI: When the mind, as the 'me', as the separate thought, puts to itself a question about itself, it has already found the answer, because it is talking about itself; it is ringing the same bell with a different hammer, but it is the same bell.

Questioner: Can we act without a 'me'? — do we not then live in contemplation?

KRISHNAMURTI: Can you live in isolation, in contemplation? Who is going to give you your food, your clothes? The monks and the various tricksters of religions have done all this. There are people in India who say, 'I live in contemplation, feed me, clothe me, bathe me, I am so disconnected' — it is all so utterly immature. You cannot possibly isolate yourself, for you are always in relationship with the past or with the things around you. To live in isolation, calling it contemplation, is mere escape, self-deception.

23rd July, 1970.

Chapter 5. FEAR AND PLEASURE

'If one is going to understand and be free of fear, one should also understand pleasure; they are interrelated.'

The last time we met we were talking about the structure of thought and its activities, about how thought divides and thereby brings about great conflict in human relationship. I think this morning we should consider — not intellectually or verbally — the nature of pleasure and fear, and whether it is at all possible to be totally free of sorrow. Enquiring into that, we have to examine very carefully the whole question of time. It is one of the most difficult things to convey something, which not only demands the accurate use of words, but also an accuracy of perception that lies beyond those words, and a feeling, a sense, of intimate contact with a reality.

In listening to the speaker, if you merely interpret the words according to your personal like and dislike, without being aware of your own tendencies of interpretation, then the word becomes a prison in which most of us, unfortunately, are caught. But if one is aware of the meaning of the word and of what lies behind the word, then communication becomes possible. Communication implies not only a verbal comprehension, but also going together, examining together, sharing together, creating together. This is very important, especially when we are talking about sorrow, time, and the nature of pleasure and fear. These are very complex questions. Every human problem is quite complex and needs a certain austerity, a simplicity, for its perception. By the word 'austere' is not meant harshness, which is the usual meaning given to that word, not the sense of dryness, of discipline and control. We mean the austere simplicity that there must be in the examination and in the understanding of what we are going to talk about. The mind must be really sensitive. Sensitivity implies intelligence which is beyond the interpretation of the intellect, beyond emotionalism and enthusiasm. In examining, in listening, in looking, in learning about time, pleasure, fear and sorrow, one has to have this quality of sensitivity which gives the immediate perception of something as true or false. That is not possible if the intellect, in its activity of thought, divides, interprets. I hope you understood, the last time we talked here, how thought, by its nature, divides human relationship — though thought is necessary, as reason, as sane, clear, objective thinking.

For most of us, fear is a constant companion; whether one is aware of it or not, it is there, hidden in some dark recess of one's mind; and we are asking if it is at all possible for the mind to be completely and totally free of this burden. The speaker may suggest this question, but it is you who must answer it, it is your problem; therefore you have to be sufficiently persistent, and sufficiently subtle, to see what it is and to pursue it to the very end, so that the mind — when you leave this tent this morning — is literally free of fear. Perhaps that is asking a great deal, but it can be done. For a mind that has been conditioned in the culture of fear, with all the neurotic, complicated consequences of its actions, to even put the question of the possibility of being completely, absolutely, free of fear, is in itself a problem. A problem exists only when it is not solvable, when you cannot go through with it and it keeps on recurring. You think you have solved this question of fear, but it keeps on repeating in different forms. If you say, 'It is impossible', you have already blocked yourself. One has to be very careful not to block oneself, not to prevent oneself from going into this question of fear and its complete resolution.

Any sense of fear generates all kinds of mischievous activity, not only psychologically and neurotically, but outwardly. The whole problem of security comes into being, both physical and psychological security. Do follow all this, because we are going to go into something which requires attention; not your agreement, not your interpretation, but your perception, your seeing the thing as it is. You do not need an interpreter; examine for yourself, find out for yourself.

Most of us have had physical fears, either fear of an illness, with all its anxiety and the boredom of pain, or when facing physical danger. When you face physical danger of any kind, is there fear? Walking in wild parts, of India or Africa or America, one may meet a bear, a snake or a tiger; then there is immediate action, not conscious deliberate action, but instinctive action. Now is that action from fear, or is that intelligence? We are trying to find an action that is intelligent, as compared with action which is born of fear. When you meet a snake, there is only instant physical response, you run away, you sweat, you try to do something about it; that is a conditioned response, because you have been told for generations to be careful of snakes, of wild animals. The brain, the nervous system, responds instinctively to protect itself; that is a natural intelligent response. To protect the physical organism is necessary; the snake is a danger and to respond to it in the sense of protection is an intelligent action.

Now look at physical pain. You have had pain previously and you are afraid that it might return. The fear is caused by thought, by thinking about something which happened a year ago, or yesterday, and which might happen again tomorrow. Go into it, watch your own responses and what your own activities have been. There, fear is the product of conscious or unconscious thought — thought as time, not chronological time, but thought as time thinking about what has happened and generating the fear of it happening again in the future. So thought is time. And thought produces fear: 'I might die tomorrow', 'I might be exposed about something I have done in the past'; the thinking about that breeds fear. You have done something which you do not want exposed, or you want to do something which you do not

48

want exposed, or you want to do something in the future which you will not be able to do; all that is the product of thought as time.

Can this movement of thought, which breeds fear in time, and as time, come to an end? Have you understood my question? There is the intelligent action of protection, of self-preservation, the physical necessity to survive, which is a natural, intelligent, response. There is the other: thought, thinking about something and projecting the possibility of it occurring, or not occurring in the future, and so breeding fear. So, the question is: can this movement of thought, so immediate, so insistent, so persuasive, naturally come to an end? Not through opposition; if you oppose it, it is still the product of thought. If you exercise your will to stop it, it is still the product of thought. If you say, 'I will not allow myself to think that way', who is the entity who says, 'I will not'? It is still thought hoping by stopping that movement, to achieve something else, which is still the product of thought. Thought may project it and may not be able to achieve it; therefore again there is fear involved.

So we are asking whether the whole activity of thought, which has produced psychological fear — not just one fear, but many, many fears — can it come to an end naturally, easily, without effort. If you make any effort it is still thought and therefore productive of fear — and it is still of time. One has to find a way in which thought will naturally come to an end and so no longer create fear.

Are we communicating with each other, not merely verbally? Perhaps you have seen the idea clearly, but we are not concerned with verbally understanding the idea, but with your involvement in fear in your daily life. We are not concerned with the description of your life; that which is described is not the actual, the explanation is not that which is explained, the word is not the thing. Your life, your fear, is not exposed by the speaker's words; but in listening, it is you who have to expose that which is fear, and see how thought creates that fear.

We are asking whether the activity of thought — which engenders, breeds, sustains and nourishes fear — can come to an end naturally without any resistance. Before we can discover the true answer, we have also to enquire into the pursuit of pleasure; because again it is thought that sustains pleasure. You may have had a lovely moment, as when you looked at the marvellous sunset yesterday, you took a great delight in it; then thought steps in and says, 'how beautiful it was, I would like to have that experience repeated again tomorrow'. It is the same whether it is a sunset, or whether somebody flatters you, whether it is a sexual experience, or if you have achieved something which you must maintain, which gives you pleasure. There is a pleasure which you derive through achievement, through being a success, the pleasure in the anticipation of what you are going to do tomorrow, from the repetition of something which you have experienced, sexually, or artistically.

Social morality is based on pleasure and therefore it is no morality at all: social morality is immorality. One finds that out; but it does not mean that by revolting against the social morality, one is going to become moral — doing what one likes, sleeping with whom one likes. If one is going to understand and be free of fear, one should also understand pleasure; they are interrelated. Which does not mean that one must give up pleasure. All the organised religions — and they have been the bane of civilisation — have said, one must have no pleasure, no sex, one must approach God as a tortured human being. They have said one must not look at a woman, or anything which might remind one of sex and so on. Saying that one must not have pleasure, means one must not have desire. So one picks up the Bible when desire arises and loses it in that; or one repeats some words from the Gita — which is nonsense.

Fear and pleasure are the two sides of a coin: you cannot be free of one without being free of the other also. You want to have pleasure all your life and yet be free of fear — that is all you are concerned about. But you do not see that you feel frustrated if tomorrow's pleasure is denied, you feel unfulfilled, angry, anxious and guilty, and all the psychological miseries arise. So you have to look at fear and pleasure together. In understanding pleasure you also have to understand what joy is. Is pleasure joy? Is not the delight of existence something totally different from pleasure?

We were asking whether thought, with all its activities which breed and sustain fear and pleasure, can come naturally to an end, without effort. There are the unconscious fears which play a much greater part in one's life than the fears of which one is aware. How are you going to uncover these unconscious fears — expose them to the light? By analysis? If you say, 'I will analyse my fears,' then who is the analyser? Is he not a part, a fragment of fear? His analysis of his own fears will therefore have no value at all. Or if you go to an analyst he, like you, is also conditioned, by Freud, Jung or Adler: he analyses according to his conditioning, therefore he does not help you to be free of fear. As we said previously, analysis is a negation of action.

Knowing analysis has no value, how are you going to uncover the unconscious fear? If you say, 'I will examine my dreams', again the same problem arises. Who is the entity that is going to examine the dreams — one fragment of the many fragments? So you must ask a quite different question which is: 'why do I dream at all'? Dreams are merely the continuation of the daily activity; there is always action going on, of some kind or another. How can that activity be understood and come to an end? That is, can the mind during the daytime be so alert as to watch all its motivations, all its urges, all its complexities, its prides, its ambitions and frustrations, its demand to fulfil, to be somebody, and so on? Can all that movement of thought during the day be watched without 'the observer'? Because if there is 'the observer' who is watching, that observer is part of thought, which has separated itself from the rest and assumed the authority to observe.

If you observe during the day the whole movement of your activities, your thoughts and feelings without interpretation, then you will see that dreams have very little meaning. Then you will hardly ever dream. If you are awake during the daytime, and not half asleep, if you are not caught in your beliefs, your prejudices, your absurd little vanities, in your petty knowledge, you will see that there will not only be the end to dreams, but also that thought itself begins to subside.

Thought is always seeking, or sustaining, or avoiding fear; it is also producing pleasure, continuing to nourish that which has been pleasurable. Being caught in fear and pleasure — which produce sorrow — how can it all come to an end? How can the machinery of thought — which produces all this movement of pleasure and fear — naturally come to an end? That is the problem. What will one do with it? Give it up, or go on as one has been, living in pleasure and pain — which is the very nature of the bourgeois mind — though you may have long hair, sleep on the bridge, revolt, throw bombs, cry 'peace' yet fight your favourite war? Do what you will, it is of the very nature of the bourgeois mind to be caught in fear and pleasure. Face it! How will you resolve this problem? You must resolve it if you want a totally different kind of life, a different kind of society, a different kind of morality; you must solve this problem. If you are young, you may say, 'It is not important', 'I will have "instant" pleasure, "instant" fear.' But all the same, it builds up and then one fine day you find yourself caught. It is your problem, and no authority can solve it for you. You have had authorities — the priests and the psychological authorities — and they have not been able to solve it; they have given you escapes, like drugs, beliefs, rituals and all the circus that goes on in the name of religion; they have offered all this to you but the basic question of fear and pleasure they have never solved. You have got to solve it. How? What are you going to do? Put your mind to this — knowing that nobody is going to solve it for you. In the realization that nobody is going to solve it for you, you are already beginning to be free of the bourgeois world.

Unless you solve this problem of fear and pleasure, sorrow is inevitable — not only your personal sorrows, but the sorrow of the world. Do you know what the sorrow of the world is? Do you know what is happening in the world? Not outwardly — all the wars, all the mischief of the politicians and so on — but inwardly, the enormous loneliness of man, the deep frustrations, the utter lack of love in this vast, uncompassionate, callous world. Unless you resolve this problem, sorrow is inevitable. And time will not solve it. You cannot say, 'I will think about it tomorrow,' 'I will have my "instant" pleasure and all the fear that comes out of it,' 'I will put up with it.' Who is going to answer you? After raising this question, seeing all the complexity of it, seeing that nobody on earth, or any divine force such as we have relied on before, is going to resolve this essential problem, how do you respond to it? What do you say, Sirs? You have no answer, have you? If you are really honest, not playing the hypocrite, or trying to avoid it, not trying to side-step when you are faced with this problem, which is the crucial problem, you have no answer. So, how are you going to find out how it can naturally come to an end? — without method, for obviously method implies time. If somebody gives you a method, a system, and you practise it, it will make your mind more and more mechanical, bring more and more conflict between 'what is' and that system. The system promises something, but the fact is you have fear; by practising the system you are moving further and further away from 'what is'; and so conflict increases, consciously or unconsciously. So what will you do?

Now, what has happened to the mind, to the brain, that has listened to all this — not merely heard a few words, but actually listened, shared, communicated, learnt? What has happened to your mind that has listened with tremendous attention to the complexity of the problem, with awareness of its own fears, and has seen how thought breeds and sustains fear as well as pleasure? What has happened to the quality of the mind that

53

has so listened? Is the quality of this mind entirely different from the moment when we began this morning, or is it the same repetitive mind, caught in pleasure and fear? Is there a new quality? Is it a mind that is not saying, 'One must put an end to fear or pleasure', but a mind that is learning by observing? Has your mind not become a little more sensitive? Before, you were just carrying this burden of fear and pleasure. By learning about the weight of the burden, have you not slightly put it aside? Have you not dropped it — and therefore you are now walking very carefully?

If you have really followed this merely by observing — not through determination or effort — your mind has become sensitive and therefore very intelligent. Next time fear arises — as it will — intelligence will respond to it, but not in terms of pleasure, of suppressing or escaping. This intelligence and sensitivity has come about by looking at this burden and putting it aside. It has become astonishingly alive; it can ask quite a different question, which is: if pleasure is not the way of life, as it has been for most of us, then is life barren? Does it mean I can never enjoy life?

Is there not a difference between pleasure and joy? You lived before in terms of pleasure and fear — the 'instant' pleasure of sex, drink, killing an animal and stuffing yourself with its meat, and all the rest of that 'pleasure'. That has been your way of life and you suddenly discover, by examining, that pleasure is not the way at all, because it leads to fear, to frustration, to misery, to sorrow, to sociological and personal disturbances and so on. So you ask quite a different question now: 'Is there joy which is untouched by thought and pleasure?' For if it is touched by thought, it again becomes pleasure and therefore fear. So having understood pleasure and fear, is there a way of daily living which is joyous — not the carrying over of pleasure and fear from day to day? To look at those mountains, the beauty of the valley, the light on the hills, the trees and the flowing river and to enjoy them! But not when you say, 'How marvellous it is,' not when thought is using it as a means of pleasure.

You can look at that mountain, the movement of a tree, or the face of a woman, or a man, and take tremendous delight in it. When you have done that, it is finished. But if you carry it over in thought, then pain and pleasure begin. Can you so look and finish with it? Be very careful, watchful, of this. Can you look at that mountain and the delight in it is enough? Not carry it over in thought to tomorrow; which means you see the danger of that. You may have some great pleasure and say, 'It is over'; yet, is it over? Is not the mind, consciously or unconsciously, thinking about it, wishing it to happen again?

So one sees that thought has nothing whatsoever to do with joy. This is a tremendous discovery for yourself — not something you have been told, not something to write about, interpreting it for somebody to read. There is a vast difference between delight, joy and bliss, on the one hand, and pleasure on the other.

I do not know if you have noticed, that the early religious pictures in the Western world avoid any kind of sensuous pleasure; there is no scenery at all, only the human body being tortured, or the Virgin Mary and so on. There is no landscape because that was pleasure, and might distract you from being concerned with the figure and its symbolism. Only much later was there the introduction of scenery, which in China and India was always part of life.

You can observe all this and find the beauty of living in which there is no effort, of living with great ecstasy, in which pleasure and thought and fear do not enter at all.

Questioner: When I dream, I sometimes see something happening in the future, which is accurate. I dreamt that I saw you come into this meeting and put the brown coat there and adjust the microphone; this was definitely a dream of what was going to happen the next morning.

KRISHNAMURTI: How do you account for that? First of all: why do you give such tremendous importance to what is going to happen in the future? Why? The astrologers, the fortune tellers, the palmists, what marvellous things they say are going to happen to you! Why are you so concerned? Why are you not concerned with the actual daily living, which contains all the treasures — you do not see it! You know, when the mind, because you have been listening here, has become somewhat sensitive — I do not say completely sensitive, but somewhat sensitive — naturally it observes more, whether of tomorrow or today. It is like looking down from an aeroplane and seeing two boats approaching from opposite directions on the same river; one sees that they are going to meet at a certain point — and that is the future. The mind, being somewhat more sensitive, becomes aware of certain things which may happen tomorrow, as well as of those which are happening now. Most of us give so much more importance to what is going to happen tomorrow and so little to what is actually happening now. And you will find, if you go into this very deeply, that nothing 'happens' at all: any 'happening' is part of life. Why do you want 'experience' at all? A mind that is sensitive, alive, full of clarity, does it need to have 'experience' at all? Please answer that question yourself.

Questioner: You tell us to observe our actions in daily life, but what is the entity that decides what to observe and when? Who decides if one should observe?

KRISHNAMURTI: Do you decide to observe? Or do you merely observe? Do you decide and say, 'I am going to observe and learn'? For then there is the question: 'Who is deciding?' Is it will that says, 'I must'? And when it fails, it chastises itself further and says, 'I must, must, must'; in that there is conflict; therefore the state of mind that has decided to observe is not observation at all.

You are walking down the road, somebody passes you by, you observe and you may say to yourself, 'How ugly he is; how he smells; I wish he would not do this or that'. You are aware of your responses to that passer-by, you are aware that you are judging, condemning or justifying; you are observing. You do not say, 'I must not judge, I must not justify'. In being aware of your responses, there is no decision at all. You see somebody who insulted you yesterday. Immediately all your hackles are up, you become nervous or anxious, you begin to dislike; be aware of your dislike, be aware of all that, do not 'decide' to be aware. Observe, and in that observation there is neither the 'observer' nor the 'observed' — there is only observation taking place. The 'observer' exists only when you accumulate in the observation; when you say, 'He is my friend because he has flattered me', or, 'He is not my friend, because he has said something ugly about me, or something true which I do not like'. That is accumulation through observation and that accumulation is the observer. When you observe without accumulation, then there is no judgement. You can do this all the time; in that observation naturally certain definite decisions are made, but the decisions are natural results, not decisions made by the observer who has accumulated.

Questioner: You said in the beginning, that the instinctive response of self-protection against a wild animal is intelligence and not fear, and that the thought which breeds fear is entirely different.

KRISHNAMURTI: Are they not different? Do you not observe the difference between thought which breeds and sustains fear, and intelligence which says 'Be careful'? Thought has created nationalism, racial prejudice, the acceptance of certain moral values; but thought does not see the danger of that. If it saw the danger, then there would be the response not of fear, but of intelligence, which would be the same as meeting the snake. In meeting the snake there is a natural self-protecting response; when meeting nationalism, which is the product of thought, which divides people and is one of the causes of war, thought does not see the danger.

26th July, 1970.

Chapter 6. THE MECHANICAL ACTIVITY OF THOUGHT

'A mind that has understood the whole movement of thought becomes extraordinarily quiet, absolutely silent.'

We were talking of the importance of thought and yet of its un-importance; of how thought has a great deal of action and within its own field only limited freedom. We spoke of a state of mind that is totally unconditioned. This morning we can go into this question of conditioning; not only the superficial, cultural con-ditioning, but also why conditioning takes place. We can enquire about the quality of mind that is not conditioned, that has gone beyond conditioning. We have to go into this matter very deeply to find out what love is. And in understanding what love is, perhaps we shall be able to comprehend the full significance of death.

So, first we will find out whether the mind can be totally and completely free of conditioning. It is fairly obvious how we are superficially conditioned by the culture, the society, the propa-ganda around us, and also by nationality, by a particular religion, by education and through environmental influences. I think it is fairly clear and fairly simple to see how most human beings, of whatever country or race, are conditioned by the particular culture or religion to which they belong. They are moulded, held within a particular pattern. One can fairly easily put aside such conditioning.

Then there is the deeper conditioning, such as an aggressive attitude towards life. Aggression implies a sense of dominance, of seeking power, possessions, prestige. One has to go very deeply to be completely free of that, because it is very subtle, taking many different forms. One may think one is not aggressive, but when one has an ideal, an opinion, an evaluation, verbal and non-verbal, there is a sense of assertiveness which gradually becomes aggressive and violent. One can see this in oneself. Behind the very word 'aggression' — though you may say it very gently — there is a kick, there is a furtive, dominant, compulsive action which becomes cruel and violent. That aggressive conditioning one has to discover, whether one has derived it from the animal, or has become aggressive in one's own self-assertive pleasure. Is one aggressive in the total sense of that word, which means 'stepping forward'?

Another form of conditioning is that of comparison. One compares oneself with what one thinks is noble or heroic, with what one would like to be, as opposed to what one is. The comparative pursuit is a form of conditioning; again, it is extraordinarily subtle. I compare myself with somebody who is a little more intelligent or more beautiful physically. Secretly or openly, there is a constant soliloquy, talking to oneself in terms of comparison. Observe this in yourself. Where there is comparison there is a form of aggression in the feeling of achievement; or, when you cannot achieve, there is a sense of frustration and a feeling of inferiority. From childhood we are educated to compare. Our educational system is based on comparison, on the giving of marks, on examinations. In comparing yourself with somebody who is cleverer, there is envy, jealousy, and all the conflict that ensues. Comparison implies measurement; I am measuring myself against something I think is better or nobler.

One asks: 'Can the mind ever be free of this social and cultural conditioning, of the mind measuring and comparing, the conditioning of fear and pleasure, of reward and punishment?' The whole of our moral and religious structures are based on this. Why is it that we are conditioned? We see the outward influences which are conditioning us and the inward voluntary demand to be conditioned. Why do we accept this conditioning? Why has the mind allowed itself to be conditioned? What is the factor behind it all? Why do I, born in a certain country and culture, calling myself a Hindu, with all the superstition and tradition imposed by the family, the society, accept such conditioning? What is the urge that lies behind this? What is the factor that is constantly demanding and acquiescing, yielding to or resisting this conditioning? One can see that one wants to be safe and secure in the community which is following a certain pattern. If one does not follow that pattern one may lose one's job, be without money, not be regarded as a respectable human being. There is a revolt against that, and that revolt forms its own conditioning — which all the young people are going through now. One must find out what is the urge that makes one conform. Unless one discovers it for oneself, one will always be conditioned one way or the other, positively or negatively. From the moment one is born until one dies, the process goes on. One may revolt against it, one may try to escape into another conditioning, withdrawing into a monastery as do the people who devote their life to contemplation, to philosophy, but it is the same movement right through. What is the machinery that is in constant movement, adjusting itself to various forms of conditioning?

Thought is everlastingly conditioned, because it is the response of the past as memory. Thought is always mechanical; it falls very easily into a pattern, into a groove, and then you consider you are being tremendously active, whether you are confined to the Communist groove, the Catholic groove, or whatever it is. It is the easiest, the most mechanical thing to do — and we think we are living! So although thought has a certain limited freedom in its field, everything it does is mechanical. After all, to go to the moon is quite mechanical, it is the outcome of the accumulated knowledge of centuries. The pursuit of technical thinking takes you to the moon, or under the sea and so on. The mind wants to follow a groove, wants to be mechanical and that way there is safety, security, there is no disturbance. To live mechanically is not only encouraged by society, but also by each one of us, because that is the easiest way to live.

So thought being a mechanical, repetitive pursuit, accepts any form of conditioning which enables it to continue in its mechanical activity. A philosopher invents a new theory, an economist a new system, and we accept that groove and follow it. Our society, our culture, our religious promptings, everything seems to function mechanically; yet in that there is a certain sense of stimulation. When you go to Mass, there is a certain excitement, emotion, and that becomes the pattern. I do not know if this is something you have ever tried — do it once and you will see the fun of it: take a piece of stick or a stone, any odd piece with a little shape to it, put it on the mantlepiece and put a flower beside it every morning. Within a month you will see that it has become a habit, as a religious symbol, and you have begun to identify yourself with that.

Thought is the response of the past. If one has been taught engineering as a profession, one adds to and adjusts that knowledge, but one is set in that line; similarly if you are a doctor and so on. Thought is somewhat free within a certain field, but it is still within the limits of mechanical functioning. Do you see that, not only verbally and intellectually, but actually? Are you as aware of it as when you hear that train? *(Sound of passing train.)*

Can the mind free itself from the habits it has cultivated, from certain opinions, judgements, attitudes and values? Which means, can the mind be free of thought? If this is not completely understood, then the next thing which I am going to talk about will have no meaning. The understanding of this leads to the next question, which is inevitable, if you go into it. If thought is mechanical, if it inevitably conforms to the conditioning of the mind, then what is love? Is love the product of thought? Is love nurtured, cultivated by thought, dependent on thought?

What is love? — bearing in mind that the description is not the described, the word is not the thing. Can the mind be free of the mechanical activity of thought so as to find out what love is? For most of us love is associated, or equated, with sex. That is a form of conditioning. When you are enquiring into this really very complex, intricate and extraordinarily beautiful thing, you must find out how that word 'sex' has conditioned the mind.

We say we will not kill — we will not go to Vietnam or some other place to kill, but we do not mind killing animals. If you yourself had to kill the animal which you eat, and saw the ugliness of it, would you eat that animal? I doubt it very much. But you do not mind the butcher killing it for you to eat; in that there is a great deal of hypocrisy.

So one asks not only what love is, but also what is compassion. In the Christian culture the animals have no soul, they are put on earth by God for you to eat; that is the Christian conditioning. In certain parts of India to kill is wrong, whether to kill a fly, an animal or anything else. So they do not kill the least thing, they go to the extreme of exaggeration; again, that is their conditioning. And there are people who support anti-vivisection, yet wear marvellous furs: such hypocrisy goes on!

What does it mean to be compassionate? Not merely verbally, but actually to be compassionate? Is compassion a matter of habit, of thought, a matter of the mechanical repetition of being kind, polite, gentle, tender? Can the mind which is caught in the activity of thought with its conditioning, its mechanical repetition, be compassionate at all? It can talk about it, it can encourage social reform, be kind to the poor heathen and so on; but is that compassion? When thought dictates, when thought is active, can there be any place for compassion? Compassion being action without motive, without self-interest, without any sense of fear, without any sense of pleasure.

So one asks: 'Is love pleasure?' — sex is pleasure, of course. We take pleasure in violence, we take pleasure in achievement, in assertion, in aggression. Also we take pleasure in being somebody. And all that is the product of thought, the product of measurement — 'I was that' and 'I will be this'. Is pleasure, in the sense in which we have been speaking, is that love? How can a mind which is caught in habit, in measurement and comparison, know what love is? One may say, love is this or that — but that is all the product of thought.

From that observation arises the question: what is death? What does it mean, to die? It must be the most marvellous experience! It must imply something that has completely come to an end. The movement that has been set going — the strife, struggle, turmoil, all the despairs and frustrations — all that suddenly comes to an end. The man who is trying to become famous, who is assertive, violent, brutal — that activity is cut off! Have you noticed how anything that continues psychologically becomes mechanical, repetitive. It is only when psychological continuance comes to an end, that there is something totally new — you can see this in yourself. Creation is not the continuation of what is, or what was, but the ending of that.

So psychologically can one die? You understand my question? Can one die to the known, die to what has been — not in order to become something else — which is the ending of and the freedom from the known? After all, that is what death is.

The physical organism will die, naturally; it has been abused, kicked around, frustrated; it has eaten and drunk all kinds of things. You know how you live and you go on that way till it dies. The body, through accident, through old age, through some disease, through the strain of constant emotional battle within and without, becomes twisted, ugly, and it dies. There is self-pity in this dying and also pity for oneself when somebody else dies. When somebody dies whom we consider we love, is there not in that sorrow a great deal of fear? For you are left alone, you are exposed to yourself, you have nobody to rely on, nobody to give you comfort. Our sorrow is tinged with this self-pity and fear and naturally in this uncertainty one accepts every form of belief.

The whole of Asia believes in reincarnation, in being reborn in another life. When you enquire what it is that is going to be reborn in the next life, you come up against difficulties. What is it? Yourself? What are you? — a lot of words, a lot of opinions, attachments to your possessions, to your furniture, to your conditioning. Is all that, which you call the soul, going to be reborn in the next life? Reincarnation implies that what you are today determines what you will be again in the next life. Therefore behave! — not tomorrow, but today, because what you do today you are going to pay for in the next life. People who believe in reincarnation do not bother about behaviour at all; it is just a matter of belief, which has no value. Incarnate today, afresh — not in the next life! Change it now completely, change with great passion, let the mind strip itself of everything, of every conditioning, every knowledge, of everything it thinks is 'right' — empty it. Then you will know what dying means; and then you will know what love is. For love is not something of the past, of thought, of culture; it is not pleasure. A mind that has understood the whole movement of thought becomes extraordinarily quiet, absolutely silent. That silence is the beginning of the new.

Questioner: Sir, can love have an object?

KRISHNAMURTI: Who is asking the question? Thought or love? Love is not asking this question. When you love, you love! — you do not ask, 'Is there an object, or no object, is it personal or impersonal?'. Oh, you do not know what is means, the beauty of it! Our love, as it is, is such a trial; our relationship with each other is such a conflict. Our love is based on your image of me and my image of you. Look at it very carefully, at the relationship between these two isolated images which say to each other, 'We love'. The images are the product of the past, of memories, memories of what you said to me and I said to you; and this relationship between the two images must inevitably be an isolating process. That is what we call relationship. To be related means to be in contact — not merely physically — which is not possible when there is an image, when there is the self-isolating process of thought, which is the 'me', and the 'you'. We say: 'Has love an object? Or is love divine or profane?' — you follow? Sir, when you love, you are neither giving nor receiving.

Questioner: When one goes behind these words, 'beauty' and 'love', don't all these divisions disappear?

KRISHNAMURTI: Have you ever sat, not day-dreaming, but very quietly, completely aware? In that awareness there is no verbalisation, no choice, no restraint or direction. When the body is completely relaxed, have you noticed the silence that comes into being? That requires a great deal of investigation, because our minds are never still but endlessly chattering and therefore divided. We divide living into fragments.

Can all this fragmentation come to an end? Knowing that thought is responsible for this fragmentation, we ask: 'Can thought be completely silent yet respond when it is necessary, without violence, objectively, sanely, rationally — still let this silence pervade?' That is the only way: to find for oneself this quality of the mind that has no fragments, that is not broken up as the 'you' and the 'me'.

Questioner: Sir, is the killing of a fly on the same level as the killing of an animal or a human being?

KRISHNAMURTI: Where will you begin the comprehension of killing? You say you will not go to war, kill a human being (I do not know if you say it or not, it is up to you), but you do not mind taking sides — your group and my group. You do not mind believing in something and standing by what you believe. You do not mind killing people with a word, with a gesture—and you will be careful not to kill a fly! Some years ago the speaker was in a country where Buddhism is the accepted religion. If you are a practising Buddhist, it is one of the accepted principles not to kill. Two people came to see the speaker and said, 'We have a problem: we do not want to kill. We are ardent Buddhists, we have been brought up not to kill; but we like eggs and we do not want to kill a fertile egg — so what are we to do?' You understand? Unless inwardly you are very clear as to what killing implies — not only with a gun, but by a word, by gesture, by division, by saying 'my country', 'your country', 'my God', 'your God', there will inevitably be killing in some form. Do not make a lot of ado about killing a fly and then go and 'kill' your neighbour with a word.

The speaker has never eaten meat in his life, does not know what it tastes like even, and yet he puts on leather shoes. One has to live, and although in your heart you do not want to kill anything, hurt anybody — and you really mean it — yet you have to 'kill' the vegetable which you eat; for if you do not eat anything you come very quickly to an end. One has to find out for oneself very clearly without any choice, without any prejudice, one has to be highly sensitive and intelligent and then let that intelligence act — not say, 'I will not kill flies', yet say something brutal about one's husband.

28th July, 1970.

Chapter 7. RELIGION

'Religion is the quality that makes for a life in which there is no fragmentation whatsoever.'

I think this morning we should talk over together the problem of religion. Many people do not like that word, they think it is rather old fashioned and has very little meaning in this modern world. And there are those who are religious at the week-end; they turn out well dressed on Sunday morning and do all the mischief they can during the week. But when we use the word 'religion' we are not in any way concerned with organised religions, churches, dogmas, rituals, or the authority of saviours, representatives of God and all the rest. We are talking about something quite different.

Human beings, in the past, as in the present, have always asked if there is something transcendental, much more real than the every-day existence with all its tiresome routine, its violence, despairs and sorrow. But not being able to find it, they have worshipped a symbol, giving it great significance.

To find out if there is something really true and sacred — I am using that word rather hesitantly — we must look for something not put together by desire and hope, by fear and longing; not dependent on environment, culture and education, but something that thought has never touched, something that is totally and incomprehensibly new. Perhaps this morning we can spend some time in enquiring into this, trying to find out whether there is a vastness, an ecstasy, a life that is unquenchable; without finding that, however virtuous, however orderly, however non-violent one is, life in itself has very little meaning. Religion — in the sense in which we are using that word, where there is no kind of fear or belief — is the quality that makes for a life in which there is no fragmentation whatsoever. If we are going to enquire into that, we must not only be free of all belief, but also we must be very clear about the distorting factor of all effort, direction and purpose. Do see the importance of this; if you are at all serious in this matter it is very important to understand how any form of effort distorts direct perception. And any form of suppression obviously also distorts, as does any form of direction born of choice, of established purpose, created by one's own desire; all these things make the mind utterly incapable of seeing things as they are.

When we are enquiring into this question of what truth is, whether there is such a thing as enlightenment, if there is something that is not of time at all, a reality that is not dependent on one's own demand, there must be freedom, and a certain quality of order. We generally associate order with discipline — discipline being conformity, imitation, adjustment, suppression and so on; forcing the mind to follow a certain course, a pattern that it considers to be moral. But order has nothing whatsoever to do with such discipline; order comes about naturally and inevitably when we understand all the disturbing factors, the disorders and conflicts going on both within ourselves and outwardly. When we are aware of this disorder, look at all the mischief, the hate, the pursuit of comparison — when we understand it then there comes order; which has nothing whatsoever to do with discipline. You must have order; after all, order is virtue (you may not like that word). Virtue is not something to be cultivated; if it is a thing of thought, of will, the result of suppression, it is no longer virtue. But if you understand the disorder of your life, the confusion, the utter meaninglessness of our existence, when you see all that very clearly, not merely intellectually and verbally, but not condemning it, not running away from it, but observing it in life, then out of that awareness and observation comes order, naturally — which is virtue. This virtue is entirely different from the virtue of society, with its respectability, the sanctions of the religions with their hypocrisy; it is entirely different from one's own self-imposed discipline.

Order must exist if we are to find out if there is — or is not — a reality that is not of time, something incorruptible, not depending on anything. If you are really serious about this, in the sense that it is a part of life as important as earning one's livelihood, as seeking pleasure, that it is something tremendously vital, then you will realize that it can only be found through meditation. The dictionary meaning of that word is to ponder over, to think over, to enquire; it means to have a mind that is capable of looking, that is intelligent, that is sane, not perverted or neurotic, not wishing for something from somewhere.

Is there any method, any system, any path which you can pursue and come to the understanding of what meditation, or the perception of reality, is? Unfortunately people come from the East with their systems, methods and so on; they say 'Do this' and 'Don't do that'. 'Practise Zen and you will find enlightenment.' Some of you may have gone to India or Japan and spent years studying, disciplining yourself, trying to become aware of your toe or your nose, practising endlessly. Or you may have repeated certain words in order to calm the mind, so that in that calmness there will be the perception of something beyond thought. These tricks can be practised by a very stupid, dull mind. I am using the word stupid in the sense of a mind that is stupefied. A stupefied mind can practise any of these tricks. You may not be interested in all this, but you have to find out. After you have listened very carefully you may go out into the world and teach people, that may be your vocation and I hope it is. You have to know the whole substance, the meaning, the fullness, the beauty, the ecstasy of all this.

A dull mind, a mind that has been stupefied by 'practising', cannot under any circumstances whatsoever understand what reality is. One must be completely, totally, free of thought. One needs a mind that is not distorted, that is very clear, that is not blunted, that is no longer pursuing a direction, a purpose. You will ask: 'Is it possible to have this state of mind in which there is no experiencing?' To 'experience' implies an entity who is experiencing; therefore, there is duality: the experiencer and the thing experienced. the observer and the thing observed. Most of us want some kind of deep, marvellous and mystical experience; our own daily experiences are so trivial, so banal, so superficial, we want something electrifying. In that bizarre thought of a marvellous experience, there is this duality of the experiencer and the experience. As long as this duality exists there must be distortion; because the experiencer is the accumulated past with all his knowledge, his memories. Being dissatisfied with that, he wants something much greater, therefore he projects it as idea, and finds that projection; in that there is still duality and distortion.

Truth is not something to be experienced. Truth is not something that you can seek out and find. It is beyond time. And thought, which is of time, cannot possibly search it out and grasp it. So one must understand very deeply this question of wanting experience. Do please see this tremendously important thing. Any form of effort, of wanting, of seeking out truth, demanding experience, is the observer wanting something transcendental and making effort; therefore the mind is not clear, pristine, non-mechanical. A mind seeking an experience, however marvellous, implies that the 'me' is seeking it — the 'me' which is the past, with all its frustrations, miseries and hopes.

Observe for yourself how the brain operates. It is the storehouse of memory, of the past. This memory is responding all the time, as like and dislike, justifying, condemning and so on; it is responding according to its conditioning, according to the culture, religion, education, which it has stored. That storehouse of memory, from which thought arises, guides most of our life. It is directing and shaping our lives every minute of every day, consciously or unconsciously; it is generating thought, the 'me', which is the very essence of thought and words. Can that brain, with its content of the old, be completely quiet — only wakened when it is necessary to operate, to function, to speak, to act, but the rest of the time completely sterile?

Meditation is to find out whether the brain, with all its activities, all its experiences, can be absolutely quiet. Not forced, because the moment you force, there again is duality, the entity that says, 'I would like to have marvellous experiences, therefore I must force my brain to be quiet' — you will never do it. But if you begin to enquire, watch, observe, listen to all the movements of thought, its conditioning, its pursuits, its fears, its pleasures, watch how the brain operates, then you will see that the brain becomes extraordinarily quiet; that quietness is not sleep but is tremendously active and therefore quiet. A big dynamo that is working perfectly, hardly makes a sound; it is only when there is friction that there is noise.

One has to find out whether one's body can sit or lie completely still, without any movement, not forced. Can the body and the brain be still? — for they are interrelated psychosomatically. There are various practices to make the body still, but again they imply suppression; the body wants to get up and walk, you insist that it must sit quietly, and the battle begins — wanting to go out and wanting to sit still.

The word 'yoga' means 'to join together'. The very words 'join together' are wrong, they imply duality. Probably yoga as a particular series of exercises and breathing was invented in India many thousands of years ago. Its intent is to keep the glands, the nerves and the whole system functioning healthily, without medicine, and highly sensitive. The body needs to be sensitive, otherwise you cannot have a clear brain. You can see the simple fact, that one needs to have a very healthy, sensitive, alert body, and a brain that functions very clearly, non-emotionally, not personally; such a brain can be absolutely quiet. Now, how is this to be brought about? How can the brain, which is so tremendously active — not only during the day-time, but when you go to sleep — be so completely relaxed and completely quiet? Obviously no method will do it, a method implies mechanical repetition, which stupefies and makes the brain dull; and in that dullness you think you have marvellous experiences!

How can the brain, which is always chattering to itself, or with others, always judging, evaluating, liking and disliking, turning over all the time — how can that brain be completely still? Do you, for yourself, see the extraordinary importance that the brain should be completely quiet? For the moment it acts it is response of the past, in terms of thought. It is only a brain that is completely still that can observe a cloud, a tree, a flowing river. You can see the extraordinary light on those mountains, yet the brain can be completely still — you have noticed this, have you not? How has that happened? The mind, facing something of extraordinary magnitude, like very complex machinery, a marvellous computer, or a magnificent sunset, becomes completely quiet even if only for a split second. You have noticed when you give a child a toy, how the toy absorbs the child, the child is so concerned with it. In the same way, by their greatness, the mountains, the beauty of a tree, the flowing waters, absorb the mind and make it still. But in that case the brain is made still by something. Can the brain be quiet without an outside factor entering into it? Not 'finding a way'. People hope for the Grace of God, they pray, have faith, become absorbed in Jesus, in this or in that. We see that this absorption by something outside occurs to a dull, a stupefied mind. The brain is active from the moment you wake up until you go to sleep; and even then the activity of the brain is still going on. That activity in the form of dreams is the same movement of the day carried on during sleep. The brain has never a moment's rest, never does it say, 'I have finished'. It has carried over the problems which it accumulated during the day into sleep; when you wake up those problems still go on — it is a vicious circle. A brain that is to be quiet must have no dreams at all; when the brain is quiet during sleep there is a totally different quality entering into the mind. How does it happen that the brain which is so tremendously, enthusiastically active, can naturally, easily, be quiet without any effort or suppression? I will show it to you.

As we said, during the day it is endlessly active. You wake up, you look out of the window and say to yourself, 'Oh, awful rain', or 'It is a marvellous day, but too hot' — you have started! So at that moment, when you look out of the window, don't say a word; not suppressing words but simply realising that by saying, 'What a lovely morning', or 'A horrible day', the brain has started. But if you watch, looking out of the window and not saying a word to yourself — which does not mean you suppress the word — just observing without the activity of the brain rushing in, there you have the clue, there you have the key. When the old brain does not respond, there is a quality of the new brain coming into being. You can observe the mountains, the river, the valleys, the shadows, the lovely trees and the marvellous clouds full of light beyond the mountains — you can look without a word, without comparing.

But it becomes much more difficult when you look at another person; there already you have established images. But just to observe! You will see when you so observe, when you see clearly, that action becomes extraordinarily vital; it becomes a complete action which is not carried over to the next minute. You understand?

One has problems, deep or superficial, not sleeping well, quarrelling with one's wife, and one carries these problems on from day to day. Dreams are the repetition of these problems, the repetition of fear and pleasure over and over again. That obviously stupefies the mind and makes the brain dull. Now is it possible to end each problem as it arises? — not carrying it over. Take a problem: somebody has insulted me, told me I am a fool; at that moment the old brain responds instantly, saying 'So are you'. If, before the brain responds, I am completely aware of what has been said — something unpleasant — I have an interval, a gap, so that the brain does not immediately jump into the battle. So if you watch the movement of thought in action during the day, you realise that it is breeding problems, and that problems are things which are incomplete, which have to be carried over. But if you watch with a brain that is fairly quiet, then you will see that action becomes complete, instantaneous; there is no carrying over of a problem, no carrying over of the insult or the praise — it is finished. Then, during sleep, the brain is no longer carrying on the old activities of the day, it has complete rest. And as the brain is quiet in sleep, there takes place a rejuvenation of its whole structure. A quality of innocency comes into being — and the innocent mind can see what is true; not the complicated mind, not that of the philosopher, or the priest.

The innocent mind implies that whole in which are the body, the heart, the brain and the mind. This innocent mind which is never touched by thought, can see what truth is, what reality is, it can see if there is something beyond measure. That is meditation. To come upon this extraordinary beauty of truth, with its ecstasy, you must lay the foundations. The foundation is the understanding of thought, which breeds fear and sustains pleasure, and the understanding of order and therefore virtue; so that there is freedom from all conflict, aggression, brutality and violence. Once one has laid this foundation of freedom, there is a sensitivity which is supreme intelligence, and the whole of the life one leads becomes entirely different.

Questioner: I think that understanding you is very important to our understanding of what you say. I was surprised to hear what you said about Yoga, how you practise it regularly two hours a day. To me this sounds like a definite form of discipline. More important than that though, is the question of innocence — I am interested in the innocence of your mind.

KRISHNAMURTI: To see the innocency of the mind, whether it is yours or mine, you must first be innocent. I am not turning the tables on you, Sir. To see the innocency of the mind you need to be free, you need to have no fear and a quality that comes with a brain that is functioning without any effort.

Is practising Yoga regularly every day for two hours, not a form of discipline? You know the body tells you when it is tired; the body says to you, 'Don't do it this morning'. When we have abused the body by driving it in all kinds of ways, spoiling its own intelligence — by wrong food, smoking, drink, all the rest of it — the body becomes insensitive. And thought says, 'I must force it'. Such driving of the body, forcing it, compelling it, becomes a discipline. Whereas, when you do these things regularly, easily, without any effort, the regularity of it depends on the sensitivity of the body. You do it one day and the next day the body may be tired and you say, 'All right, I won't do it'. It is not a mechanical regularity. All this requires a certain intelligence, not only of the mind, but of the body, and that intelligence will tell you what to do and what not to do.

Questioner: We may want our minds to be quiet, but sometimes we have to take decisions; this makes for difficulty and causes problems.

KRISHNAMURTI: If the mind cannot decide clearly, then problems arise; the very decision is a problem. When you decide, you make a decision between this and that — which means choice. When there is choice there is conflict; from that arise problems. But when you see very clearly, there is no choice, therefore there is no decision. You know the way from here to where you happen to live very well; you follow the road which is very clear. You have been on that road a hundred times, therefore there is no choice, although you may find a short-cut which you may take next time. That is something mechanical, there is no problem. The brain wants the same thing to happen again so that it may function automatically, mechanically, so that problems do not arise. The brain demands that it operate mechanically. Therefore it says, 'I will discipline myself to function mechanically', 'I must have a belief, a purpose, a direction, so that I can set a path and follow it'; and it follows that groove.

76

What happens? Life will not allow that, there are all kinds of things happening; so thought resists, builds a wall of belief and this very resistance creates problems.

When you have to decide between this and that, it means there is confusion: 'should I, or should I not do this?' I only put that question to myself when I do not see clearly what is to be done. We choose out of confusion, not out of clarity. The moment you are clear your action is complete.

Questioner: But it cannot always be complete.

KRISHNAMURTI: Why not?

Questioner: Often it is a complex choice and you have to take time, you have to look at it.

KRISHNAMURTI: Yes Sir, take time, have patience to look at it. You have to compare — compare what? Compare two materials, blue and white; you question whether you like this colour or that colour, whether you should go up this hill or that hill. You decide. 'I prefer to go up this hill today and tomorrow I'll go up the other'. The problem arises when one is dealing with the psyche, what to do within oneself. First watch what decision implies. To decide to do this or that, what is that decision based on? On choice, obviously. Should I do this, or should I do that? I realise that when there is choice there is confusion. So I see the truth of this, the fact, the 'what is', which is: where there is choice there must be confusion. Now why am I confused? Because I don't know, or because I prefer one thing as opposed to another which is more pleasant, it may produce better results, greater fortune, or whatever it is. So I choose that. But in following that, I realise there is also frustration in it, which is pain. So I am caught again between fear and pleasure. Seeing I am caught in this, I ask, 'Can I act without choice?' That means: I have to be aware of all the implications of confusion and all the implications of decision; for there is duality, the 'decider' and the thing decided upon. And therefore there is conflict and perpetuation of confusion.

You will say, to be aware of all the intricacies of this movement will take time. Will it take time? Or can it be seen instantly and therefore there is instant action? It only takes time when I am not aware of it. My brain, being conditioned, says, 'I must decide' — decide according to the past; that is its habit. 'I must decide what is right, what is wrong, what is duty, what is responsibility, what is love'. The decisions of the brain breed more conflict — which is what the politicians throughout the world are doing. Now, can that brain be quiet, so that it sees the problem of confusion instantly, and acts because it is clear? Then there is no decision at all.

Questioner: Can we learn from experience?

KRISHNAMURTI: Certainly not. Learning implies freedom, curiosity, enquiry. When a child learns something, he is curious about it, he wants to know, it is a free momentum; not a momentum of having acquired and of moving from that acquisition. We have innumerable experiences; we have had five thousand years of wars. We have not learnt a thing from them except to invent more deadly machinery with which to kill each other. We have had many experiences with our friends, with our wives, with our husbands, with our nation — we have not learnt. Learning, in fact, can only take place when there is freedom from experience. When you discover something new, your mind must be free of the old, obviously. For this reason, meditation is the emptying of the mind of the known as experience; because truth is not something that you invent, it is something totally new, it is not in terms of the past 'known'. Its newness is not the opposite of the old; it is something incredibly new: a mind that comes to it with experience cannot see it.

30th July, 1970.

78

PART II

DIALOGUES

Dialogue 1

The need to know oneself. Knowing and learning: learning needs a mind free of the past. Escaping from fear and learning about fear. The difficulty of looking at fear. Who is looking?

KRISHNAMURTI: We are going to have seven discussions here, in which each one of us shares. It is not merely a matter of hearing a few words from each other and holding onto our opinions and judgments; but in discussing, in talking things over together, we will begin to find out for ourselves how we think, from what point of view we look at life, how formulas and conclusions sway or control our minds. During these seven discussions we can go into many problems, taking each morning a particular subject and going into it as completely and as thoroughly as possible so that both of us understand it entirely, not only verbally, intellectually (which of course is not understanding) and go beyond it. So what shall we take this morning?

Questioner (1): Shall we talk about the roots and origin of thought?

Questioner (2): Could we go into the difference between the mind and the brain?

Questioner (3): Can one find a system of meditation in oneself or is it a method?

Questioner (4): Do we make the right use of our personal faculties and capacities?

Questioner (5): Could you say something about relationship between people?

Questioner (6): Could we discuss letting go and giving up all conditioning?

Questioner (7): What is enlightenment?

Questioner (8): Why is it so difficult for us to attain a state of bliss based on truth and beauty?

KRISHNAMURTI: Can we put all these questions together? I think if we could discuss what self-knowledge is, wouldn't all these questions be answered? Such questions as: what is meditation — is it a system? What is the difference between the mind and the brain? Why is it so difficult to attain or understand what is enlightenment? Why is it that most of us have to struggle in various forms? Could we take self-knowing in which all this would be included? Is there a method or system by which one can know oneself? Is there a way of finding out for oneself the answer to all the questions that we have put this morning without asking anybody? That is possible only if I know for myself the mechanism of thought, how the brain works, how the mind is caught in conditioning, how it is attached, how it wants to free itself. There is a constant struggle within oneself and also outwardly. So to answer all the questions that one puts to oneself and to solve the problems that exist outwardly, is it not important to understand oneself? Could we discuss this?

First of all how do I observe myself? Do I look at myself according to what authorities, the specialists, the psychologists have said, which has obviously conditioned my mind? I may not like Freud, Jung, Adler and the more recent psychologists and analysts, but as their very statements have penetrated into my mind, I am looking at myself with their eyes. Can I look at myself objectively without any emotional reaction, just to see what I am? And to see what I am, is analysis necessary?

All these questions are involved when I say that I must know myself; without knowing myself completely I have no basis for any action. If I don't know myself and am confused, whatever action I take must lead to further confusion. So I *must* know myself. I must profoundly find out the structure of my nature. I have to see the scaffold of my activities, the patterns in which I function, the lines which I follow, the directions which I have established for myself or society. I have to understand this drive which makes me do things consistently or contradictorily. To understand all these problems about whether there is a God, whether there is truth, what meditation is, who is the meditator — which is much more important than meditation — I must know myself completely. Do you see the importance of knowing for yourself what you are? Because without knowing yourself, whatever you do will be done in ignorance, therefore in illusion, in contradiction: so there will be confusion, sorrow and all the rest of it. Is that clear? One must know oneself not only at the conscious level but in the deep layers of oneself. This must be clear and you must know it for yourself — not because I say so.

Now, how shall I know myself? What is the procedure? Shall I follow the authorities, the specialists who apparently have investigated and have come to certain conclusions which later psychologists or philosophers may alter or strengthen? Don't say 'No'. If I don't, how shall I understand myself? All the investigations of the past philosophers and teachers — the Indian mind has gone into this at great depth — as well as of the modern ones is imprinted on my mind, consciously or unconsciously. So shall I follow because I am just beginning and they have gone ahead of me and then go further than they have gone? Or won't I follow anybody but look at myself? If I can look at myself as 'what is', then I am looking at myself who is the result of all the sayings of these philosophers, teachers and saviours. Therefore I don't have to follow anybody. Is this clear? Do see this, please, don't come back to it later.

My mind is the result of what they have said. It has not only been accepted; these things have flowed in like a wave, not only from the present but also from the past and through a great many teachers. I am the result of all that. So all that I have to do is to observe myself, read the book which is myself. How am I to read, how am I to observe so clearly that there is no impediment? I may have coloured glasses, I may have certain prejudices, certain conclusions which will prevent me from looking at myself and seeing all that is implied in looking at myself. So what shall I do? As I am conditioned I cannot look at myself in complete freedom, therefore I must be aware of my conditioning. So I have to ask: What is it to be aware?

Now let's proceed. I cannot look at myself wholly in freedom because my mind isn't free. I have a dozen opinions and conclusions, an infinite number of experiences, I have had an education — all that is part of my conditioning; therefore I must be aware of these conditionings which are part of me. So first I must know, I must understand, what it means to be aware. What does it mean to you to be aware? The other day the speaker said 'Don't take notes, please' — you heard that and several people went on taking notes. Is that to be aware?

Questioner: I know already that I can't be aware for more than two minutes and then disorder begins.

KRISHNAMURTI: We will come to whether this awareness can be extended or is only possible for a very short period. But before we answer that question let's find out what it means to be aware. Am I aware of the noise of that stream? Am I aware of all the different colours the men and women wear in this tent? Am I aware of the structure and shape of the tent? Am I aware of the space around the tent, the hills, the trees, the clouds, the heat — am I objectively, outwardly aware of all these things? How are you aware?

Questioner: We are aware inwardly and outwardly at the same time.

KRISHNAMURTI: Please go step by step. Are you aware of this tent, of the various colours of the people's dresses, are you aware of the hills, the trees, the meadows? Are you aware in the sense of being conscious of it? You are — aren't you?

Questioner: When I put my attention on it I am aware of it.

KRISHNAMURTI: When you put your attention on it you are aware. Therefore you are not aware when you are inattentive. So

83

only when you pay attention, are you aware. Please follow this closely.

Questioner: When I pay attention to one thing, I am absorbed, I cannot pay attention to the other things around me.

KRISHNAMURTI: You become absorbed in one particular thing and the rest fades away. Are you aware that when you are looking attentively at the tent, the trees, the mountains, that you are shaping into words what you see? You say, 'That's a tree, that's a cloud, that's a tent, I like this colour, I don't like that colour' — right? Please take a little trouble over this — don't get bored. Because if you go into this very deeply, when you leave the tent you will see something for yourself. So when you watch, are you aware of your reactions?

Questioner: It seems as if attention expands.

KRISHNAMURTI: I am asking something and you reply to something else. I am aware of that dress. My reaction says, 'How nice' or 'How ugly'. I am asking: when you look at that red colour are you aware of your reactions? Not of a dozen reactions, but of that particular reaction when you see a red colour? Why not? Isn't that part of awareness?

Questioner: When you put a name to a thing you are not aware.

KRISHNAMURTI: I am going to find out Sir, what it means. You don't bite into this! I want to be aware and I know I am not aware. Occasionally I am attentive, but most of the time I am half asleep. I am thinking about something else whilst I am looking at a tree or a colour. As I have said, I want to know myself completely because I see that if I don't know myself I have no basis to do anything. So I *must* know myself. How do I become aware, how do I observe myself? In observing I shall learn. So learning is part of awareness. Am I going to learn about myself according to somebody else? — according to the philosophers, the teachers, the saviours, the priests? Is that learning? If I learn according to what others have said I have stopped learning about myself, haven't I? So the first thing is, I have to learn about myself. Now what does this learning about myself mean? Investigate it, go into it, find out what it means — to learn about oneself.

Questioner: Seeing my reaction.

KRISHNAMURTI: No, Madame, I don't mean that. What does it mean to learn?

Questioner: It seems that one desperately looks for a practical system to come to such an awareness. At one time I thought we could try to educate ourselves by writing down all our thoughts and afterwards when reading them, see them like a film. Maybe in this way we could learn something.

KRISHNAMURTI: The questioner says, we see the reason for knowing ourselves, we are desperate to find out how to do this, but out of this desperation we want a system, to find some method, because we don't know what to do with ourselves. So we want somebody to tell us, 'Do these things and you will know yourself'.

Now Sirs, please do listen to me. Here I am: I am the result of the society, of the culture in which I live, of religions, the business world, the economic world, the climate, the food — I am the result of all that, of the infinite past and of the present. I want to know myself, that is, I want to learn about myself. What does the word 'learn' mean? See the difficulty in this. I don't know German, which means I have to learn the meaning of words, memorize the verbs, and learn the syntax. That is, I have to accumulate knowledge of words and all the rest of it and then I may be able to speak German. I accumulate and then act, verbally or in any other way; there learning meant accumulation. Now what happens if I learn about myself? I see something about myself and I say, 'I have learnt that'. I have seen 'that is so', I have learnt about it. That has left a residue of knowledge and with that knowledge I examine the next incident. And that again adds further accumulation. So the more I observe myself and learn about myself, the more I am accumulating knowledge about myself. Right?

Questioner: I am changing.

KRISHNAMURTI: I am accumulating knowledge and in the process I am changing. But I am accumulating knowledge and experience by observing. Now what happens? With that knowledge I look at myself. So knowledge is preventing fresh observation. I don't know if you see this? For instance you have said something to hurt me. That is my knowledge, and the next time I see you, that knowledge of having been hurt comes forward to meet you. The past comes to meet the present. So knowledge is the past and with the eyes of the past I am looking at the present — do you understand? Now, to learn about myself, to look at myself, there must be freedom from past knowledge. That is, the learning about myself must be constantly fresh. Do you see the difficulty?

Questioner: I would say there are constants in life which don't change.

KRISHNAMURTI: We'll come to the problem of change later. I am watching, I want to learn about myself. 'Myself' is movement, 'myself' is not static, it's living, active, going in different directions. So if I learn with the mind and the brain that is the past, that prevents me from learning about myself. If you once see that, then the next question is: how is the mind to free itself from the past so as to learn about itself, which is constantly new? See the beauty of it, the excitement of it!

I want to learn about myself and 'myself' is a living thing, not something dead. I think this way one day, and the next day I want something else; this is a living constant, moving thing. And to observe, to learn about it, the mind must be free. Therefore if it is burdened with the past it cannot observe. So what is it to do?

Questioner: It is not a question of amnesia, but of being free from the effects of the past.

KRISHNAMURTI: Yes Sir, that is what we mean. Now what shall I do? I see this happen: I see that red colour and I say, 'I don't like it'. That is, the past responds. The past acts immediately and therefore stops learning. So what is one to do?

Questioner: One must forget how to think — not have thoughts.

KRISHNAMURTI: You are not following what I am saying. You have come to a conclusion when you say 'not to have thoughts'. You are not really learning.

Questioner: We have to empty ourselves.

KRISHNAMURTI: That is another conclusion. How do you empty yourself? Who is the entity that is going to empty the mind?

Questioner: You have to empty that too. You must empty everything.

KRISHNAMURTI: Who is going to empty it? You see Sir, you are not listening to what is being said — if you will forgive me for saying so. I said I want to learn about myself. I cannot learn about myself if the past interferes. Learning implies the active present of the word to learn; 'learning' means active in the present; and that is not possible when the mind, when the brain, is burdened with all the past. Now tell me what to do.'

Questioner: I have to be attentive.

KRISHNAMURTI: You see! How am I to be attentive?

Questioner: I have to live in the present.

KRISHNAMURTI: How am I to live in the present when my past is burdening me?

Questioner: By being aware of the process that is taking place.

KRISHNAMURTI: Which means what? To be aware that the past is interfering and therefore preventing the brain from learning? Go slowly, Sir. Are you aware of this movement as we are talking? Then, if you are aware of it as we are talking, what takes place? Don't guess! Don't say 'should be', 'should not be' — that has no meaning. What is actually taking place when you are aware of this movement, which is the past interfering with the present and therefore preventing learning in the sense we are using that word? When you are aware of this whole process going on what takes place then?

Questioner: You see yourself as the effect of the past.

KRISHNAMURTI: We see that is a fact. We have asked what is the outcome, what happens when you are aware that you are the effect of the past and that is preventing you from learning in the present? Don't guess. What takes place in you, when you are aware of this process?

Questioner (1): The movement stops.
Questioner (2): There is no more thought.
Questioner (3): There is fear.

88

KRISHNAMURTI: One says there is no more thought, another says there is silence, yet another says there is fear.

Questioner: There seems to be nothing but the present.

KRISHNAMURTI: Now which of these statements is true?

Questioner: We are confused.

KRISHNAMURTI: That's right, we are confused.

Questioner (1): You are aware.
Questioner (2): You learn.
Questioner (3): I feel that there is a contradiction which has to be destroyed by direct action.

KRISHNAMURTI: Look Sirs, I beg of you, don't come to any conclusion, because conclusions will prevent you from learning. And if you say, 'Direct action must happen' that is a conclusion. We are learning. I see that I am the effect of the past. The past may be yesterday or the last second that has left a mark as knowledge. That knowledge, which is the past, is preventing me from learning in the present; it is a momentum, it is happening all the time. Now when I am aware of this movement, what takes place? I don't want your conclusions. If I accept your conclusions, you will be the new philosopher! I don't want any new philosopher! I want to learn; therefore what I have to see is what actually takes place when the brain is aware of this movement. Can the brain be aware of this movement or is it frightened to be aware of something new?

Questioner: The movement will stop.

KRISHNAMURTI: Then what? Have I learnt? Is there a learning?

Questioner: If I am quiet enough I think I can see what I perceive and what comes out from myself.

KRISHNAMURTI: Yes Sir, please do observe this. I want to learn about this movement; to learn I must have curiosity. If I merely come to a conclusion my curiosity stops. So there must be curiosity to learn; there must be passion, and there must be energy. Without this I can't learn. If I have fear I have no passion. So I have to leave that alone and ask: why am I frightened to learn about something that may be new? I have to investigate fear. I have left the momentum of the past and am now going to learn about fear. Are you following all this? Now, why am I frightened?

Questioner: We are afraid to lose the image of ourselves.

KRISHNAMURTI: I am afraid to lose the image which I have built about myself — who is full of knowledge, who is a dead entity. No Sir. Don't give me the explanation. I realise I am frightened — why? Is it because I see that I am dead? I am living in the past and I don't know what it means to observe and live in the present; therefore this is something totally new and I am frightened to do anything new. Which means what? That my brain and my mind have followed the old pattern, the old method, the old way of thinking, living and working. But to learn, the mind must be free from the past — we have established that as the truth. Now, look what has happened. I have established the fact as truth that there is no learning if the past interferes. And also I realise that I am frightened. So there is a contradiction between the realisation that to learn, the mind must be free of the past, and that at the same time I am frightened to do so. In this there is duality. I see, and I am afraid to see.

Questioner: Are we always afraid to see new things?

KRISHNAMURTI: Aren't we? Aren't we afraid of change?

Questioner: The new is the unknown. We are afraid of the unknown.

KRISHNAMURTI: So we cling to the old and this will inevitably breed fear because life is changing; there are social upheavals, there is rioting, there are wars. So there is fear. Now how am I to learn about fear? We have moved away from the previous movement; now we want to learn about the movement of fear.

What is the movement of fear? Are you aware that you are afraid? Are you aware that you have fears?

Questioner: Not always.

KRISHNAMURTI: Sir, do you know *now,* are you aware of your fears now? You can resuscitate them, bring them out and say, 'I am afraid of what people might say about me'. So are you aware that you are frightened about death, about losing money, about losing your wife? Are you aware of those fears? Also of physical fears — that you might have pain tomorrow and so on. If you are aware, what is the movement in it? What takes place when you are aware that you are afraid?

Questioner: I try to get rid of it.

KRISHNAMURTI: When you try to get rid of it, what takes place?

Questioner: You repress it.

KRISHNAMURTI: Either you repress it or escape from it; there is a conflict between fear and wanting to get rid of it — isn't there? So there is either repression or escape; and in trying to get rid of it there is conflict which only increases fear.

Questioner: May I ask a question? Isn't the 'me' the brain itself? The brain gets tired of always seeking new experiences and wants relaxation.

KRISHNAMURTI: Are you saying that the brain itself is frightened to let go and is the cause of fear? Look Sir, I want to learn about fear; that means I must be curious, I must be passionate. First of all I must be curious and I cannot be curious if I form a conclusion. So to learn about fear I mustn't be distracted by running away from it; there mustn't be a movement of repression, which again means a distraction from fear. There mustn't be the feeling 'I must get rid of it'. If I have these feelings I cannot learn. Now have I these feelings when I see there is fear? I am not saying you shouldn't have these feelings — they are there. If I am aware of them what shall I do? My fears are so strong that I want to run away from them. And the very movement away from them breeds more fear — are you following all this? Do I see the truth and the fact that moving away from fear increases fear? Therefore there is no movement away from it — right?

Questioner: I don't understand this, because I feel that if I have a fear and I move away from it, I am moving towards something that is going to end that fear, towards something that will see me through it.

KRISHNAMURTI: What are you afraid of?

Questioner: Money.

KRISHNAMURTI: You are afraid of losing money, not of money. The more the merrier! But you are afraid of losing it — right? Therefore what do you do? You make quite sure that your money is well placed, but the fear continues. It may not be safe in this changing world, the bank may go bankrupt and so on. Even though you have plenty of money there is always this fear. Running away from that fear doesn't solve it, nor suppressing it, saying, 'I won't think about it': for the next second you *are* thinking about it. So running away from it, avoiding it, doing anything about it continues fear. That is a fact. Now we have established two facts: that to learn there must be curiosity and there must be no pressure of the past. And to learn about fear there must be no running away from fear. That is a fact; that is the truth. Therefore *you don't run away*. Now when I don't run away from it what takes place?

Questioner: I stop being identified with it.

KRISHNAMURTI: Is that what learning is? You have stopped.

Questioner: I don't know what you mean.

KRISHNAMURTI: Stopping is not learning. Because of the desire not to have fear, you want to escape from it. Just see the subtlety of it. I am afraid, and I want to learn about it. I don't know what is going to happen, I want to learn the movement of fear. So what takes place? I am not running away, I am not suppressing, I am not avoiding it: I want to learn about it.

Questioner: I think about how to get rid of it.

KRISHNAMURTI: If you want to get rid of it — as I have just explained — who is the person who is going to get rid of it? You want to get rid of it, which means you resist it — therefore fear increases. If you don't see the fact of that, I am sorry I can't help you.

Questioner: We must accept fear.

KRISHNAMURTI: I don't accept fear — who is the entity who is accepting fear?

Questioner: If one cannot escape, one must accept.

KRISHNAMURTI: To escape from it, to avoid it, to pick up a novel and read what other people are doing, to look at television, go to the temple or to church — all that is still avoidance of fear, and any avoidance of it only increases and strengthens fear. That is a fact. After establishing that fact I won't run away, I won't suppress. I am learning not running away. Therefore what takes place when there's an awareness of fear?

Questioner: Understanding of the process of fear.

KRISHNAMURTI: We are doing it. I am understanding the process, I am watching it, I am learning about it. I am afraid

93

and I am not running away from it — now what takes place?

Questioner: You are face to face with fear.

KRISHNAMURTI: What takes place then?

Questioner: There is no movement in any direction.

KRISHNAMURTI: Don't you ask this question? Please just listen to me for two minutes. I am not running away, I am not suppressing, I am not avoiding, I am not resisting it. There it is, I am watching it. The natural question arising out of that is: who is watching this fear? Please don't guess. When you say, 'I am watching fear, I am learning about fear', who is the entity that is watching it?

Questioner: Fear itself.

 Difference between Concluding and knowing

KRISHNAMURTI: Is fear itself watching itself? Please don't guess. Don't come to any conclusion, find out. The mind isn't escaping from fear, not building a wall against fear through courage and all the rest of it. What takes place when I watch? I ask myself naturally: who is watching the thing called fear? Don't answer me please. I have raised the question, not you. Sir, find out who is watching this fear: another fragment of me?

Questioner: The entity who is watching cannot be the result of the past, it must be fresh — something that happens at this moment.

KRISHNAMURTI: I am not talking about whether the watching is the result of the past. I am watching, I am aware of fear, I am aware that I am frightened of losing money, of becoming ill, of my wife leaving me and God knows what else. And I want to learn about it, therefore I am watching and my natural question is: who is watching this fear?

Questioner: My image of myself.

KRISHNAMURTI: When I ask the question: 'who is watching', what takes place? — in the very question there is a division,

94

isn't there? That is a fact. When I say, 'Who is watching,' it means the thing is there and I am watching, therefore there is a division. Now why is there a division? You answer me this, don't guess, don't repeat what somebody else has said, including myself. Find out why this division exists at the moment when you ask the question: 'who is watching'? Find out.

Questioner: There is a desire on my part to watch.

KRISHNAMURTI: Which means the desire says, 'Watch in order to escape' — you follow? You said before, 'I have understood that I mustn't escape', and now you find that desire is making you escape subtly; therefore you are still watching fear as an outsider. See the importance of this. You are watching with an intention to get rid of fear. And we said a few minutes ago, to try to get rid of fear means first censoring fear. So your watching implies trying to get rid of fear; therefore there is a division which only strengthens fear. So I am again asking the question: who is watching fear?

Questioner: Isn't there also another point: who is asking the the question 'who is watching fear'?

KRISHNAMURTI: I am asking that question Sir.

Questioner: But who is asking the question?

KRISHNAMURTI: The same thing, only you push it further back. Now please listen: this is the most practical way of going about it. You will see if you follow this very carefully that the mind will be free of fear, but you are not doing it.

I am frightened of losing money and therefore what do I do? I escape by avoiding thinking about it. So I realise how silly it is to avoid it, because the more I resist it the more I am afraid. I am watching it and the question arises: who is watching it? Is it the desire that wants to get rid of it, go beyond it, be free

95

of it, that is watching? *It is*. And I know watching it that way only divides and therefore strengthens fear. So I see the truth of that, therefore desire to get rid of it has gone — you follow me? It's like seeing a poisonous snake: the desire to touch it is finished with. The desire to take drugs is finished when I see the real danger of them; I won't touch them. As long as I don't see the danger of it, I'll go on. In the same way, as long as I don't see that running away from fear strengthens fear, I'll go on running away. The moment I see it I won't run. Then what happens?

Questioner: How can a person look who is afraid of being involved? One is scared.

KRISHNAMURTI: I am pointing it out to you. The moment you are scared of looking at fear, you won't learn about it, and if you want to learn about fear, don't be scared. It is as simple as that. If I don't know how to swim I won't plunge into the river. When I know that fear cannot possibly be ended if I am afraid to look — and if I really want to look — I'll say, 'I don't care, I'll look'.

Questioner: It was said, it is desire to get away from fear that constantly breeds more fear. When I'm afraid I want to get away from it, so what I always do is to let it be relative so that I can identify with it, so that I can unify myself.

KRISHNAMURTI: You see that! It is all these tricks that we are playing on ourselves. Do listen Sir. Who is saying all this? You make an effort to identify yourself with fear.

Questioner: I am that fear.

KRISHNAMURTI: Ah! Wait. If you are that fear, as you say you are, then what happens?

Questioner: When I come to terms with it, it begins to diminish.

KRISHNAMURTI: No. Not coming to terms! When you say that you *are* fear, fear is not something separate from you. What takes place? I am brown. I am afraid to be brown, but I say, 'Yes, I am brown' and that's the end of it, isn't it? I am not running away from it. What takes place then?

Questioner: Acceptance.

KRISHNAMURTI: Do I accept it? On the contrary, I forget that I am brown. You don't even know all this, you are just guessing.

I want to learn about myself. I must know myself completely, passionately, because that is the foundation of all action; without that I'll lead a life of utter confusion. To learn about myself I cannot follow anybody. If I follow anybody I am not learning. Learning implies that the past does not interfere, because 'myself' is something extraordinary, vital, moving, dynamic; so I must look at it afresh with a new mind. There is no new mind if the past is always operating. That is a fact, I see that. Then in seeing that I realise I am frightened. I don't know what will happen. So I want to learn about fear — you follow? I am moving all the time in the movement of learning. I want to know about myself and I realise something — a profound truth. I am going to learn about fear, which means I mustn't run away from it *at any price*. I mustn't have a subtle form of desire to run away from it. So what happens to a mind that is capable of looking at fear without division? The division being, trying to get rid of it, subtle forms of escape, suppression and so on; what happens to the mind when it is confronted with fear and there is no question of running away from it? Please find out, give your mind to it.

2nd August, 1970

Dialogue 2

Recapitulation. Fears prevent mature growth. Do we see *the effects of fear or only know about them? The difference between fear as a memory and actual contact with fear. Dependence and attachment caused by fear of man's emptiness and nothingness. Uncovering loneliness and shallowness. The futility of escapes. 'Who is aware of the emptiness?'*

KRISHNAMURTI: Yesterday we were talking about fear and the necessity of knowing oneself. I don't know if one sees the great importance of understanding the nature and structure of oneself. As we said, if there is no comprehension, not intellectual or verbal, but an actual understanding of what one is and the possibility of going beyond it, we must inevitably bring about confusion and contradiction in ourselves, with activities that will lead to a great deal of mischief and sorrow. So it is absolutely essential that one should understand, not only the superficial layers of oneself, but the total entity, all the hidden parts. And I hope in communicating with each other, in understanding this whole problem together, we shall be able to see, actually, not theoretically, if through self-knowledge the mind can go beyond its own conditioning, its own habits, its own prejudices and so on.

We were also talking about learning about oneself. Learning implies a non-accumulative movement; there is no movement if there is accumulation. If the flowing river ends up in a lake there is no movement. There is movement only when there is a constant flow, a strong current. And learning implies that; learning not only about outward things and scientific facts, but also learning about oneself, because 'oneself' is a constantly changing, dynamic, volatile being. To learn about it past experiences in no way help; on the contrary, the past puts an end to learning and therefore to any complete action. I hope we saw this very clearly: that we are dealing with a constantly living

98

movement of life, a movement which is the 'me'. To understand that 'me', which is so very subtle, there needs to be an intense curiosity, a persistent awareness, a sense of non-accumulative comprehension. I hope we are able to communicate with each other about this whole question of learning.

That is where our trouble is going to be, because our mind likes to function in grooves, in patterns, from a fixed conclusion or a prejudice, or from knowledge. The mind is tethered to a particular belief and from there it tries to understand this extra-ordinary movement of the 'me'. Therefore there is a contradiction between the 'me' and the observer.

We were also talking about fear, which is part of this total movement of the 'me'; the 'me' which breaks up life as a movement, the 'me' which separates itself as the 'you' and the 'me'. We asked, 'What is fear?' We are going to learn non-accumulatively about fear; the very word 'fear' prevents coming into contact with that feeling of danger which we call fear. Look, Sirs, maturity implies a total, natural development of a human being; natural in the sense of non-contradictory, harmonious — which has nothing to do with age. And the factor of fear prevents this natural, total development of the mind. I'll go on a little and then we will discuss all this.

When one is afraid, not only of physical things, but also of psychological factors, in that fear what takes place? I am afraid; not only of physically falling ill, of dying, of darkness — you know the innumerable fears one has, both biological as well as psychological. What does that fear do to the mind, the mind which has created these fears? Do you understand my question? Don't answer me immediately, look at yourselves. What is the effect of fear on the mind, on one's whole life? Or are we so used to fear, have we accustomed ourselves to fear, which has become a habit, that we are unaware of its effect? If I have accustomed myself to the national feeling of the Hindu, to the dogma, to the beliefs, I am enclosed in this conditioning and totally unaware of what the effects of it are. I only see the feeling that is aroused in me, the nationalism, and I am satisfied with that. I identify myself with the country, with the belief and all the rest of it. But we don't see the effect of such a conditioning all around. In the same way, we don't see what fear does — psychosomatically, as well as psychologically. What does it do? Sirs, this is a discussion, you have to take part in it!

Questioner: I become involved in trying to stop this thing from happening.

KRISHNAMURTI: It stops or immobilizes action. Is one aware of that? Are you? Don't generalise. We are having all these discussions in order to see what is actually happening within us; otherwise these dialogues have no meaning. In talking over what fear does and becoming conscious of it, it might be possible to go beyond it. So if I am at all serious I must see the effects of fear. Do I know the effects of it? Or do I only know them verbally? Do I know them as something which has happened in the past, which remains a memory and that memory says: 'These are the effects of it'? So that memory sees the effects of it, but the mind doesn't see the actual effect. I don't know if you see this? I have said something which is really quite important.

Questioner: Could you say it again?

KRISHNAMURTI: When I say I know the effects of fear, what does that mean? Either I know it verbally, that is intellectually, and I know it as a memory, as something that has happened in the past, and I say: 'This did happen'. So the past tells me what the effects are. But I don't see the effects of it at the actual moment. Therefore it is something remembered and not real. Whereas 'knowing' implies non-accumulative seeing — not recognition — but seeing the fact. Have I conveyed this?

When I say 'I am hungry', is it the remembrance of having been hungry yesterday which tells me, or is it the actual fact of

100

hunger *now*? The actual awareness that I am hungry now, is entirely different from the response of a memory which tells me I have been hungry and therefore I may be hungry now. Is the past telling you the effects of fear, or are you aware of the actual happening of the effects of fear? The actions of the two are entirely different — aren't they? The one, being completely aware of the effects of fear now, acts instantly. But if memory tells me these are the effects, then the action is different. Have I made myself clear? Now, which is it?

Questioner: Can you distinguish between a particular fear and actually being aware of the effects of fear as such — *apart from remembering the effects of a fear?*

KRISHNAMURTI: That's what I was trying to explain. The action of the two are entirely different. Do you see that? Please, if you don't see it don't say 'yes', don't let's play games with each other. It is very important to understand this. Is the past telling you the effects of fear, or is there a direct perception or awareness of the effects of fear *now*? If the past is telling you the effects of fear, the action is incomplete and therefore contradictory; it brings conflict. But if one is completely aware of the effects of fear *now,* the action is total.

Questioner: As I am sitting in the tent now I have no fear because I am listening to what you are talking about, so I am not afraid. But this fear may come up as I leave the tent.

KRISHNAMURTI: But can't you, sitting here in this tent, see fear, which you may have had yesterday, can't you invoke it, invite it?

Questioner: It may be life fears.

KRISHNAMURTI: Whatever the fear may be, need you say, 'I have no fears now, but when I go outside I'll have them'. They are there!

Questioner: You can invoke it — as you say — you can remember it. But this is the point you made about bringing in memory, the thought about fear.

KRISHNAMURTI: I am asking: need I wait until I leave the tent to find out what my fears are? Or, sitting here, can I be aware of them? I am not afraid at this moment of what someone might say to me. But when I meet the man who is going to say these things, that will frighten me. Can't I see the actual fact of that now?

Questioner: If you do that, you are already making a practice of it.

KRISHNAMURTI: No, it is not a practice. You see, you are so afraid of doing anything which might become a practice! Sir, aren't you afraid of losing your job? Aren't you afraid of death? Aren't you afraid of not being able to fulfil? Aren't you afraid of being lonely? Aren't you afraid of not being loved? Don't you have some form of fear?

Questioner: Only if there is a challenge.

KRISHNAMURTI: But I *am* challenging you! I can't understand this mentality!

Questioner: If there is an impulse you act, you have to do something.

KRISHNAMURTI: No! You are making it so complicated. It is as natural as hearing that train roar by. Either you can remember the noise of that train, or listen actually to that noise. Don't complicate it, please.

Questioner: Aren't you in a way complicating it by talking about invoking fear? I don't have to invoke any of my fears — just by being here I can survey my reaction.

KRISHNAMURTI: That's all I am saying.

Questioner: In order to communicate here we must know the difference between the brain and the mind.

KRISHNAMURTI: We have discussed that before. We are now trying to find out what fear is, learn about it. Is the mind free to learn about fear? Learning being watching the movement of fear. You can only watch the movement of fear, when you are not remembering past fears and watching with those memories. Do you see the difference? I can watch the movement. Are you learning about what is actually taking place when there is fear? We are boiling with fear all the time. We don't seem to be able to get rid of it. When you had fears in the past and were aware of them, what effect had those fears on you and on your environment? What happened? Weren't you cut off from others? Weren't the effects of those fears isolating you?

Questioner: It crippled me.

KRISHNAMURTI: It made you feel desperate, you didn't know what to do. Now, when there was this isolation, what happened to action?

Questioner: It was fragmentary.

KRISHNAMURTI: Do listen to this carefully please. I have had fear in the past and the effects of those fears were to isolate me, to cripple me, to make me feel desperate. There was a feeling of running away, of seeking comfort in something. All that we will call for the moment isolating oneself from all relationship. The effect of that isolation in action is to bring about fragmentation. Didn't this happen to you? When you were frightened you didn't know what to do, you ran away from it, or tried to suppress it, or reason it away. And when you had to act you were acting from a fear which is in itself isolating. So an action born out of that fear must be fragmentary. Fragmentation being contradictory, there was a great deal of struggle, pain, anxiety — no?

Questioner: Sir, as a crippled person walks on crutches, so a person who is numbed, crippled by fear, uses various kinds of crutches.

KRISHNAMURTI: That's what we are saying. That's right. Now you are very clear about the effect of past fear: it produces fragmentary actions. What is the difference between that and the action of fear without the response of memory? When you meet physical danger what takes place?

Questioner: Spontaneous action.

KRISHNAMURTI: It is called spontaneous action — is it spontaneous? Please do enquire, we are trying to find out something. You are in the woods by yourself, in some wild part, and suddenly you come upon a bear with cubs — what happens then? Knowing the bear is a dangerous animal what happens to you?

Questioner: The adrenalin is increased.

KRISHNAMURTI: Yes, now what is the action that takes place?

Questioner: You see the danger of transmitting your own fear to the bear.

KRISHNAMURTI: No, what happens *to you?* Of course if you are afraid you transmit it to the bear and the bear gets frightened and attacks you. This is all very simple, you are missing the whole point. Have you ever faced a bear in the woods?

104

Questioner: There is someone here who has.

KRISHNAMURTI: I have. That gentleman and I have had many of these experiences during certain years. But what takes place? There is a bear a few feet away from you. There are all the bodily reactions, the flow of adrenalin and so on; you stop instantly and you turn away and run. What has happened there? What was the response? A conditioned response, wasn't it? People have told you generation after generation, 'Be careful of wild animals'. If you get frightened you will transmit that fear to the animal and then he will attack you. The whole thing is gone through instantly. Is that the functioning of fear — or is it intelligence? What is operating? Is it fear that has been aroused by the repetition of: 'be careful of the wild animals', which has been your conditioning from childhood? Or is it intelligence? The conditioned response to that animal and the action of that conditioned response is one thing. The operation of intelligence and the action of intelligence is different; the two are entirely different. Are you meeting this? A bus is rushing by, you don't throw yourself in front of it; your intelligence says, 'Don't do it'. This is not fear — unless you are neurotic or have taken drugs. Your intelligence, not fear, prevents you.

Questioner: Sir, when you meet a wild animal don't you have to have both intelligence and a conditioned response?

KRISHNAMURTI: No Sir. See it. The moment it is a conditioned response there is fear involved in it and that is transmitted to the animal; but not if it is intelligence. So find out for yourself which is operating. If it is fear then its action is incomplete and therefore there is a danger from the animal; but in the action of intelligence there is no fear at all.

Questioner (1): You are saying that if I watch the bear with this intelligence, I can be killed by the bear without experiencing fear.

Questioner (2): If I hadn't met a bear before, I wouldn't even know it was a bear.

KRISHNAMURTI: You are all making such complications. This is so simple. Now leave the animals alone. Let us start with ourselves; we are partly animals too.

The effects of fear and its actions based on past memories are destructive, contradictory and paralysing. Do we see that? — not verbally but actually; that when you are afraid you are completely isolated and any action that takes place from that isolation must be fragmentary and therefore contradictory, therefore there is struggle, pain and all the rest of it. Now, an action of awareness of fear without all the responses of memory is a complete action. Try it! Do it! Become aware as you are walking alone when you go home; your old fears will come up. Then watch, be aware whether those fears are actual fears, or projected by thought as memory. As the fear arises watch whether you are watching from the response of thought, or whether you are merely watching. What we are talking about is action, because life is action. We are not saying only one part of life is action. The whole of living is action and that action is broken up; the breaking up of action is this process of memory with its thoughts and isolation. Is that clear?

Questioner: You mean the idea is to experience totally every split second, without memory entering?

KRISHNAMURTI: Sir, when you put a question like that, you have to investigate the question of memory. You have to have memory, the clearer, the more definite, the better. If you are to function technologically, or even if you want to get home, you have to have memory. But thought as the response of memory, and projecting fear out of that memory, is an action which is entirely different.

Now, what is fear? How does it happen that there is fear? How do these fears take place? Would you tell me please?

106

Questioner: In me it is the attachment to the past.

KRISHNAMURTI: Let's take that one thing. What do you mean by that word 'attachment'?

Questioner: The mind is holding on to something.

KRISHNAMURTI: That is, the mind is holding on to some memory. 'When I was young, how lovely everything was.' Or, I am holding on to something that might happen; so I have cultivated a belief which will protect me. I am attached to a memory, I am attached to a piece of furniture, I am attached to what I am writing because through writing I will become famous. I am attached to a name, to a family, to a house, to various memories and so on. I have identified myself with all that. Why does this attachment take place?

Questioner: Isn't it because fear is the very basis of our civilisation?

KRISHNAMURTI: No Sir; why are you attached? What does that word attachment signify? I depend upon something. I depend on you all attending, so that I can talk to you; I am depending on you and therefore I am attached to you, because through that attachment I gain a certain energy, a certain *élan,* and all the rest of that rubbish! So I am attached — which means what? I depend on you; I depend on the furniture. In being attached to the furniture, to a belief, to a book, to the family, to a wife, I am dependent on that to give me comfort, to give me prestige, social position. So dependence is a form of attachment. Now why do I depend? Don't answer me, look at it in yourself. You depend on something, don't you? On your country, on your gods, on your beliefs, on the drugs you take, on drink!

Questioner: It is part of social conditioning.

KRISHNAMURTI: Is it social conditioning that makes you

depend? Which means you are part of society; society is not independent of you. You have made society which is corrupt, you have put it together. In that cage you are caught, you are part of it. So don't blame society. Do you see the implications of dependency? What is involved? Why are you depending?

Questioner: So as not to feel lonely.

KRISHNAMURTI: Wait, listen quietly. I depend on something because that something fills my emptiness. I depend on knowledge, on books, because that covers my emptiness, my shallowness, my stupidity; so knowledge becomes extraordinarily important. I talk about the beauty of pictures because in myself I depend on that. So dependence indicates my emptiness, my loneliness, my insufficiency and that makes me depend on you. That is a fact isn't it? Don't theorise, don't argue with it, it is so. If I were not empty, if I were not insufficient, I wouldn't care what you said or did. I wouldn't depend on anything. Because I am empty and lonely I don't know what to do with my life. I write a stupid book and that fills my vanity. So I depend, which means I am afraid of being lonely, I am afraid of my emptiness. Therefore I fill it with material things or with ideas, or with persons.

Aren't you afraid of uncovering your loneliness? Have you uncovered your loneliness, your insufficiency, your emptiness? That is taking place now, isn't it? Therefore you are afraid of that emptiness *now.* What are you going to do? What is taking place? Before, you were attached to people, to ideas, to all kinds of things and you see that dependence covers your emptiness, your shallowness. When you see that, you are free — aren't you? Now what is the response? Is that fear the response of memory? Or is that fear actual, do you see it?

I work hard for you, don't I? *(Laughter)* There was a cartoon yesterday morning: a little boy says to another boy, 'When I grow up I am going to be a great prophet, I am going

108

to speak of profound truths but nobody will listen'. And the other little boy says, 'Then why will you talk, if nobody is going to listen?' 'Ah', he said, 'us prophets are very obstinate'. (*Laughter*)

So now you have uncovered your fear through attachment, which is dependency. When you look into it you see your emptiness, your shallowness, your pettiness and you are frightened of it. What takes place then? See it Sirs?

Questioner: I try to escape.

KRISHNAMURTI: You try to escape through attachment, through dependency. Therefore you are back again in the old pattern. But if you see the truth that attachment and dependency cover your emptiness, you won't escape, will you? If you don't see the fact of that, you are bound to run away. You will try to fill that emptiness in other ways. Before, you filled it with drugs, now you fill it with sex or with something else. So when you see the fact of that, what has happened? Proceed Sirs, go on with it! I have been attached to the house, to my wife, to books, to my writing, to becoming famous; I see fear arises because I don't know what to do with my emptiness and therefore I depend, therefore I am attached. What do I do when I get this feeling of great emptiness in me?

Questioner. There is a strong feeling.

KRISHNAMURTI: Which is fear. I discover I am frightened, therefore I am attached. Is that fear the response of memory, or is that fear an actual discovery? Discovery is something entirely different from the response of the past. Now which is it with you? Is it the actual discovery? Or the response of the past? Don't answer me. Find out, Sir, dig into yourself.

Questioner: Sir, in that emptiness surely there is openness towards the world?

KRISHNAMURTI: No, I am asking something entirely different. The fear of emptiness, of loneliness and all that insufficiency — which you have not been able to understand sufficiently to go through with it and finish it — has brought about fear. Is it your discovery *now,* here in the tent? Or is it recognition of the past? Have you discovered that you are attached because you depend, and that you depend because of fear of emptiness? Are you aware of your emptiness and of the process this implies? Becoming aware of that emptiness, is there fear involved in it or are you merely empty? Do you merely see the fact that you are lonely?

Questioner: If you can see that, you are not alone any more.

KRISHNAMURTI: We'll go step by step if you don't mind. Do you see that? Or are you going back to the old dependency, the old attachment, to the regular pattern being repeated over and over again? What is going to take place?

Questioner: Sir, isn't this the whole human predicament — I don't think I am as well off as a small dog, who hasn't got all these problems.

KRISHNAMURTI: Unfortunately we are not dogs. I am asking something which you don't answer. Have you discovered for yourself the fear that takes place when you see your emptiness, your shallowness, your isolation? Or, having discovered it are you going to run away, get attached to something? If you don't run away through dependency and attachment, then what takes place when there is this emptiness?

Questioner: Freedom.

KRISHNAMURTI: Do look at it, it's quite a complex problem, don't say it is freedom. Before, I was attached and I covered

110

up my fear. Now, by asking that question, I discover this at-tachment was an escape from the fear which came into being when I was aware of my emptiness for a split second. Now I have finished with running away. Then what takes place?

Questioner: I was going to say that after that split second there is another escape.

KRISHNAMURTI: Which means you don't see the futility of escapes. Therefore you keep on escaping. But if you *do* see, if you are aware of your emptiness, what takes place? If you are watching very carefully, what generally takes place is, you ask: 'who is aware of this emptiness?'.

Questioner: The mind.

KRISHNAMURTI: Please don't jump into it. Go step by step. Who is aware of it? The mind? A part of the mind is aware of another part which is lonely? Do you see my question? I have suddenly become aware that I am lonely. Is it a fragment of my mind which says 'I am lonely?' In that there is a division. As long as there is a division there is an escape. You don't see this!

Questioner: What happens when you experience the emptiness? When you experience this loneliness, you are no longer aware of it.

KRISHNAMURTI: Look Sir. Please listen. You need here a per-sistent observation, not any conclusion, or anything that you think should be. That is, I am aware of my emptiness. Before, I have covered it up, now it has been stripped and I am aware. Who is aware of this emptiness? A separate segment of my mind? If it is, then there is a division between emptiness and the thing that is aware that it is empty; then what takes place in that emptiness, in that division? I can't do anything about it. I want to do something about it and I say, 'I must bring it together', 'I must experience this emptiness', 'I must act'. As long as there is a division between the observer and the observed, there is contradiction and therefore there is conflict. Is that what you are doing? A separate segment of the mind watching an emptiness which is not part of itself? Which is it? Sirs, you have to answer this! If it is a part that is watching, then what is that part?

Questioner: Is it intelligence born out of energy?

KRISHNAMURTI: Don't complicate it, it is complex enough. Don't bring in other words. My question is very simple. I asked: when you are aware of this emptiness from which you have escaped through attachment, and you are no longer running away from it, who is aware? It is for you to find out.

Questioner: This awareness that you are empty is another escape and you see you are nothing else but all these things put together.

KRISHNAMURTI: When you say, "I am aware of my emptiness" it is another form of escape and we are caught in a network of escapes. That's our life. If you realise that attachment is an escape, then you drop that escape. Are you going from one escape to another? Or do you see one factor of escape and therefore you have understood all the factors of escape?

Sirs, you cannot possibly sustain a continuous watchfulness for more than ten minutes and we have talked for an hour and fifty minutes. So we had better stop. We will continue with the same thing tomorrow, until it becomes *real* to you — not because I say so; it's your life.

3rd August 1970.

Dialogue 3

The depths of dependence and fear. Watching attachment; levels of attachment. Habit. Need to see the total network of habits. How can one see totally? The difference between analysis and observation. The mechanism behind habit. What is creativeness?

KRISHNAMURTI: Yesterday we were talking about dependency, its attachments and fear. I think this may be an important issue in our life, so we should really go into it rather deeply. After all, one can see that freedom cannot possibly exist when there is any form of dependency. There is physiological and psychological dependence, the biological dependence on food, clothes and shelter, which is a natural dependency. But there is an attachment that arises through the biological necessity, like having a house to which one is psychologically attached; or one is attached to certain forms of food, or to compulsive eating, because of other factors of fear which have not been discovered, — and so on.

There are physical dependencies of which one can fairly easily be aware, like depending on smoking, on drugs, on drink, on various forms of physical stimulations on which one depends psychologically. Then there are the psychological dependencies. One has to watch this very carefully, because they flow into each other, they are inter-related. There is dependence on a person, or a belief, or on an established relationship, on a psychological habit of thought. I think one can be aware of all this fairly easily. And because there is dependence and attachment, both physical or psychological, the fear of losing that to which one is attached brings about fear.

One may depend on belief, or on an experience, or on a conclusion attached to a particular prejudice; how deeply does this attachment go? I do not know if you have observed it in yourself. We were watching it all throughout the day, to find out if there is any form of attachment — coming here regularly, living in a particular chalet, going to one country after another, talking, addressing people, being looked up to, criticised, exposed. If one has watched throughout the day, one discovers naturally how deeply one is attached to something, or to someone, or not at all. If there is any form of attachment — it doesn't matter what it is — to a book, to a particular diet, to a particular pattern of thought, to a certain social responsibility — such attachment invariably breeds fear. And a mind that is frightened, though it may not know it is because it is attached, obviously is not free and must therefore live in a constant state of conflict.

One may have a particular gift, like a musician, who is tremendously attached to his instrument or to the cultivation of his voice. And when the instrument or the voice fails, he is completely lost, his days are ended. He may insure his hands or his fiddle, or he can become a conductor, but he knows through attachment the inevitable darkness of fear is waiting.

I wonder if each one of us — if we are at all serious — has gone into this question, because freedom means freedom from all attachment and therefore from all dependency. A mind that is attached is not objective, not clear, cannot think sanely and observe directly.

There are the superficial, psychological attachments and there are deep layers in which there may be some form of attachment. How do you discover those? How does the mind, which may consciously observe its many attachments and realise the nature of those attachments, see the truth and the implications of that truth? It may have other forms of hidden attachments. How are you going to uncover those concealed, secret attachments? A mind that is attached goes through the conflict of realising it must be detached, otherwise it suffers pain and then gets attached to something else and so on. This is our life. I find I am attached to my wife and I may see all the consequences of it. Being attached to her I realise there must inevitably be fear involved in it. Therefore there is the conflict of detachment and the trial of relationship, the conflict in relationship. That is fairly easy to observe clearly and expose to oneself.

Our question is, how deeply is one attached to some form of tradition in the hidden recesses of one's mind, whatever it is. Please follow, because you will see freedom implies complete freedom from all this, otherwise there must be fear. And a mind that is burdened with fear is incapable of understanding, of seeing things as they are and going beyond them.

How does one observe the hidden attachments? I may be stubborn, thinking I am not attached; I may have come to the conclusion that I am not depending on anything. That conclusion makes for stubbornness. But if one is learning, seeking, watching, then in that act of learning there is no conclusion. Most of us are attached to some form of conclusion and according to that conclusion we function. Can the mind be free from forming conclusions? — all the time, not just occasionally.

'I like long hair, I don't like long hair', 'I like this, I don't like that'. Intellectually, or through some experience, you have come to a way of thinking, whatever it is. Can the mind act without conclusion? That is one point. Secondly can the mind reveal to itself the hidden attachments, patterns and dependencies? And thirdly, seeing the nature and structure of attachment, can the mind move within a way of life which is not isolating but highly active and yet not fixed at any point. We'll go into it.

First of all, are we aware that we are biologically, physically and psychologically attached. Are you aware that you are physically attached to things? And are you also aware of the implications of those attachments? If you are attached to smoking, see how extraordinarily difficult it is to give it up. For the people who smoke — to whom it has become a habit — it is incredibly difficult; not only does it act as a stimulant, a social habit, but there is the attachment to it. Is one aware of the attachment to drinks, to drugs, to various forms of stimuli? If you are, can you drop it instantly?

Suppose I am attached to whiskey and I am aware of that. It has become a tremendous habit, the body demands it, it has got used to it, it can't do without it. And you have come to the conclusion that you musn't drink, it is bad for you, the doctors have asked you to cut it down. But the body and the mind have fallen into the habit of it. Watching this habit, can the mind drop it completely, immediately? See what is involved in it. The body demands it because it has got into the habit, and the mind has said, 'I must give it up'. So there is a battle between the bodily demands and the decision of the mind. What are you going to do? Instead of whiskey, take your own habits; perhaps you don't drink whiskey, but you have other physiological habits, like frowning, watching with your mouth open, fiddling with your fingers. Please, Sir, let's discuss this. The body is attached to drink and the mind says, 'I must be free of it'; and also you realise that when there is conflict between the body and the mind it becomes a problem, a struggle. What will you do? Please, Sirs, come on! You must be extraordinarily free of all habits, if you can't discuss this!

Questioner: Either you stop it or you go on drinking.

KRISHNAMURTI: What do you actually do? Please don't play with this, because if you once understand it, you will see how extraordinarily vital it becomes, how important it becomes to act, to be without any form of effort, which means, without any distortion.

Questioner: I realise that I am my habit.

KRISHNAMURTI: Yes. Then what will you do? I realise I am my habit, my habit is me.

Questioner (1): Must we not go to the roots of these habits?
Questioner (2): We must begin by stopping resistance to it.

KRISHNAMURTI: Sir, may I say something? Don't let's theorise, don't let's speculate. Don't tell me what to do, but let us find out, let us learn not only how to look, but how from that very looking action takes place.

I have a particular habit of scratching my head, fiddling with my fingers, watching things with my mouth open, very physical things. Now how do I bring it to an end without the least effort? We are discussing habits to which we are attached, consciously or unconsciously. I am taking the most trivial habits, like scratching my head, or pulling my ears, or fiddling with my fingers. How does the mind stop it without any kind of effort, knowing that effort implies duality, implies resistance, condemnation, a desire to go beyond it — when I either suppress or escape, verbally or non-verbally. So bearing all that in mind, understanding those facts, how do I stop a physical habit without effort?

Questioner: You observe it in its entirety.

KRISHNAMURTI: Wait, Sir, that statement may answer all our questions. You observe it in its entirety. What does that mean? Not just *one* habit, like scratching, or fiddling with your fingers, but the whole mechanism of habits. The *whole* of it, not a fragment of it. Now, how does the mind watch the whole of the habits in which it lives?

Questioner: With passive awareness or passive observation.

KRISHNAMURTI: You are quoting the speaker. I'm afraid that won't do. Don't quote anybody, Sir!

Questioner: Is it the mind forming the habit?

KRISHNAMURTI: Do look, Sir, that question is really quite important, if you go into it. Can the mind watch, not only a particular little habit, but be aware of this whole mechanism of forming habits. Please don't say yes, don't come to any conclusion. Look what is implied in this question. There are not only small habits like fiddling with one's fingers, but also sexual habits, habits of patterns of thought, various activities. I think this, I conclude this, and that has become a habit. I live in habits, my whole life is a structure of habits. How is the mind to be aware of the entire mechanism of habit?

One has a thousand and one habits, the way you brush your teeth, comb your hair, the way you read, the way you walk. One of the habits is wanting to become famous, wanting to become important. How is the mind to become aware of all these habits? Is it to become aware of one habit after another? Do you know how long that would take? I could spend the rest of my days watching each habit and yet not solve it. I'm going to learn about it, I'm going to find out, I'm not going to leave it. I am asking, is it possible for the mind to see the whole network of habits? How is it to do it? Don't guess, don't come to a conclusion, don't offer an explanation — I'm not interested, it doesn't mean a thing to say, 'Go and do something'. I want to learn about it *now*. What do I do?

Questioner: Can one be aware of the waste of energy in pursuing a particular pattern of habit — or many patterns — and thereby liberate oneself?

KRISHNAMURTI: I've come to all of you and I say: Please help me to find this out. I'm hungry, don't give me a menu, but give me food! I am asking: what will you do?

Questioner: Understand one habit, totally, then possibly one could discard all habits.

KRISHNAMURTI: How do I watch one habit, which is twiddling my fingers, and see all the other habits? Is that possible with such a small affair? I know I do it because of tension. I can't get on with my wife, and so I develop this peculiar habit, or I do it because I am nervous, shy, or this or that. But I want to learn about the whole network of habits. Am I to do it bit by bit, or is there a way of looking at this whole network instantly? Please answer me.

Questioner: The structure of habits consists of two parts . . . .

KRISHNAMURTI: There are two parts, the habits, and the observer who is concerned with those habits. And the observer is also a habit. So both are habits. I fiddle with my fingers and the observation comes from an entity which is also the result of habits. Obviously! So it is all habits. Please, Sirs, how will you help me, teach me, to learn about it?

Questioner: My whole life is habit, my mind is a habit, it is the state of mind that I have to change.

KRISHNAMURTI: Who is the 'I' that is going to change it? The 'I' is also a habit, the 'I' is a series of words and memories and knowledge, which is the past, which is a habit.

Questioner: As we are all caught in habits, we obviously don't know.

KRISHNAMURTI: Therefore why don't you say, 'I don't know', instead of throwing in a lot of words? If you don't know, then let's learn together. But first be clear that you don't know; and don't quote anybody. Are we in the position to say, 'I really don't know'?

Questioner: But why do we have these habits?

KRISHNAMURTI: It's fairly simple. If I have a dozen habits, get up every morning at eight o'clock, go to the office, come back home at six o'clock, take a drink, and so on, I don't have to think very much, be alive very much. The mind likes to function in grooves, in habits: it is safe, secure. That doesn't need a great deal of explanation. Now how is the mind to observe this whole network of habits?

119

Questioner: Maybe we can pay attention every moment, as far as our energies allow.

KRISHNAMURTI: You see, that is just an idea. I am not interested. Sir, you made a statement, which was: can the mind see the whole structure and nature of the mechanism of habit and when it sees the totality, there may be a different action. That's what we are enquiring into — may I go into it now? We are going to find out together.

How is the mind, including the brain, to see something totally? — not only habit, but see anything totally. We see things fragmentarily, don't we? Business, family, community, individuals, my opinion and your opinion, my God, your God — we see everything in fragments. Isn't that a fact? Are you aware of it? If the seeing is fragmentary, then you cannot see the totality. If I see life in fragments because my mind is conditioned, then obviously it cannot see the totality of the human being. If I separate myself through my ambition, through my particular prejudices, I cannot see the whole. Am I aware that I am looking at life partially — the 'me' and the 'not-me', 'we' and 'they'? Do I look at life that way? If I do, then obviously I can't see anything totally. Then arises my question: how is the mind, which is so caught up in this habit of a fragmentary outlook and activity, to see the whole? Obviously it can't. If I am concerned with my particular fulfilment, ambition, competition and my desire to achieve, I can't see the whole of mankind. So what am I to do? Wanting to fulfil, wanting to be somebody, wanting to achieve something is a habit: a social habit as well as a habit that gives me pleasure. When I go down the street people look at me and say, 'There he goes'. That gives me great pleasure. As long as the mind is operating in that field of fragmentation, obviously it can't see the whole. Now my question is: what is the mind to do, functioning in fragments and realising that it cannot possibly see the whole? Is it to break down every fragment, understand every fragment? That would take a long time.

Are you waiting for an answer from the speaker?

Questioner: There must be total silence.

KRISHNAMURTI: Oh, he is quoting somebody.

Questioner: If we could see all our habits right now, as they are really happening and see the process which is preventing us from seeing this actually now . . .

KRISHNAMURTI: We are doing that, aren't we? You don't go any further, you go back over and over again. I am caught in a habit *now;* I fiddle with my fingers, I listen to what is being said with my mouth open and I see that it is habit; my question is: can I understand this whole machinery of habit now. You don't pay attention. Look, Sir, a mind that is in fragments cannot possibly see the whole. So I take one habit and through learning about that one habit, I see the whole mechanism of all habits. What habit shall I take?

Questioner: Smoking . . . .

KRISHNAMURTI: All right. I am not analysing: — do you understand the difference between analysis and observation? Analysis implies the one who analyses and the thing to be analysed. The thing to be analysed is smoking and to analyse that, there must be an analyser. The difference between analysis and observation is this: observation is seeing directly, without analysis, seeing without the observer, seeing the red, pink, or black dress as it is, without saying I don't like it. Do you follow? In seeing there is no observer. I see the colour red and there is no like or dislike, there is observation. Analysis implies, 'I don't like red because my mother who quarrelled with my father . . .' taking it back to my childhood. So analysis implies an analyser. Please realise that there is a division between the analyser and the thing analysed. In observation there is no division. There is observation without the censor, without saying, 'I like', 'I don't like', 'this is beautiful', 'this is not beautiful', 'this is mine', 'this is not mine'. You have to do this, not just theorise about it, then you'll find out.

As I said, we are not analysing, we are merely observing the habit of smoking. In observing, what is revealed? — not your interpretation of what it shows. Do you see the difference? There is no interpretation, there is no translation, no justification, no condemnation. What does the habit of smoking reveal?

Questioner: It reveals that you are drawing smoke into your lungs.

KRISHNAMURTI: That is one fact. Second, what does it tell you? It is going to tell you the history of smoking, if you don't interpret. If you can listen, if you can watch smoking, the picture is going to tell you all it wants.

Now what does it tell you? — that you are drawing a lot of smoke into your lungs? What else?

Questioner: That you are dependent.

KRISHNAMURTI: Is shows you that you are dependent on a weed.

Questioner: That inside you are empty.

KRISHNAMURTI: That is your translation. What does it tell *you*?

Questioner: I see that it is just a mechanical thing, I don't think much about it — I just do it.

KRISHNAMURTI: It tells you that you are doing something mechanically. It tells you that when you first smoked it made you sick; it was not pleasant, but as other people did it, so you did it. Now it has become a habit.

Questioner: Doesn't it tell you that it tranquillises you to a certain extent?

122

KRISHNAMURTI: It tells you that it puts you to sleep, helps you to drug yourself, it quietens your nerves, cuts your appetite, so that you don't get fat.

Questioner: It tells you you are bored with life.

KRISHNAMURTI: It tells you that it makes you relax when you meet others and feel nervous. It has told you a lot.

Questioner: It tells me that I am inattentive.

KRISHNAMURTI: That is your translation — it is not telling you that you are inattentive.

Questioner: It gives me a certain satisfaction, especially after supper.

KRISHNAMURTI: Yes, it helps you, it is telling you all this. And why are you doing it? Just listen, Sir — don't answer me so quickly please. Why are you accepting all that it has revealed to you? Television tells you what to do, what kind of soap to buy and all the rest of it. You have all seen those commercials! You are being told all the time — why do you accept it? The sacred books tell you what you should do and what you should not do. Why do you accept the propaganda of churches or politicians?

Questioner: Because it is easier to follow a system.

KRISHNAMURTI: Why do you follow it? Is it for the sake of security? To feel companionship with others? To be like the rest of the people? Which means, you are frightened not to be like other people. You want to be like everybody else, because in that there is perfect safety. If you are a non-Catholic in a Catholic country you find it very difficult. If you are in a Communist country and don't follow the party-line, you'll find it difficult.

Now look what the picture of that weed has revealed and why I am caught in the habit. It is the inter-relationship between the cigarette and me. This is habit, this is the way my whole mind is working: I do something because it is safe. I get into a habit — trivial or important — because I don't have to think about it any more. So my mind feels that it is safe to function in habits. I see the whole mechanism of this habit-formation. Through the one habit of smoking, I have discovered the whole pattern; I have discovered the machinery that is producing habits.

Questioner: I didn't quite understand how through listening to one habit you can see the whole mechanism of habit.

KRISHNAMURTI: I've shown it to you, Sir. Habit implies functioning mechanically and from the observation of the mechanical habit of smoking, I see how the mind functions in habits.

Questioner: But are all habits mechanical?

KRISHNAMURTI: They must be — the moment you use the word habit, it must be mechanical.

Questioner: Aren't there deeper dependencies than just mechanical habits?

KRISHNAMURTI: The moment we use the word habit, it implies mechanical repetition — establishing a habit — which means doing the same thing over and over again. So there is no good or bad habit: we are concerned only with habit.

Questioner: If I have the habit of power, or the habit of comfort for instance, or the habit of property, isn't that something deeper than just a mechanical habit?

KRISHNAMURTI: The habit of power, the demand for power, position, domination, aggression, violence — all that is implied in the desire for power. To do what one wants to do, like a child, or like a grown-up man; that has become a habit.

Questioner: Or wanting security . . .

KRISHNAMURTI: I said it gives you safety and so on. In examining that one habit I have seen that all the other habits are based on that. Since habits are mechanical, repetitive, when I say, 'I would like to be a great man', then I become caught because in that habit I find security and I pursue that. Deepdown — we are not discussing good or bad habits, only habit — all habits are mechanical. Anything that I do repetitively, which is doing something from yesterday to today to tomorrow, must be mechanical. Some mechanical action may have a little more polish, function a little more smoothly, but it is still habit, is still repetitive — that's obvious.

Questioner: Would you say that certain creative efforts are habits?

KRISHNAMURTI: Let's answer that question. Would you say creativeness is a habit?

Questioner: Creativity implies freshness. One can't make an effort to be creative.

KRISHNAMURTI: Are you saying all this because you are creative or are you just guessing at it? One has to ask what you mean by creativeness. This is a tremendous question — and you brush it aside. You paint a picture; either you do it because you love painting, or because it brings you money, or you want to find some original way of painting and so on. What does it mean to be creative? A man who writes a poem because he can't get on with his wife or with society, is he creative? The man who is attached to his violin and makes a lot of money out of it, is he creative? And the man who is in great tension in himself, and

125

out of that tension produces plays of which the world says, 'How marvellous' — would you call that creative? The man who drinks and out of that writes a marvellous poem full of rhythm — is he creative?

Questioner: How can you judge?

KRISHNAMURTI: I am not judging.

Questioner: But that is the question you pose. If I say someone is or isn't creative, I am judging.

KRISHNAMURTI: I am not judging, Sir, I am asking, I am learning, I look at all the people who write books, who write poems or plays, who play the violin. I see this in front of me, I don't say: this is good, this is bad; I say: what is creativeness? The moment I say, 'This is right' I am finished, then I can't learn. And I want to learn, I want to find out what it means to be creative.

Questioner: Perhaps it is to have an innocent universality . . .

KRISHNAMURTI: I don't know — perhaps — I want to find out, I want to learn.

Questioner: It is to be alive.

KRISHNAMURTI: I go to a museum and see all those pictures, admire them, compare them and I say, 'What marvellously creative people they are'. So I want to find out what it is to be creative. Must I write a poem, paint a picture, write a play, to be creative? Which means, does creativeness demand expression? Please listen carefully. Is the woman who bakes bread in a hot kitchen creative?

Questioner: We generally call these activities creative.

KRISHNAMURTI: I am questioning it. I don't say they are not — I don't know. I want to learn.

126

Questioner: If I make bread — and I have never done it before — I'm creative.

KRISHNAMURTI: I am asking you, Sir, what is creativeness.

Questioner: We are creative at this moment.

KRISHNAMURTI: No, no. Observing all the things man has called creative I ask myself, what is creativeness? Must it have an expression? — like baking bread, painting a picture, writing a play, making money. Does it demand expression?

Questioner: Yes, I think we are being creative now.

KRISHNAMURTI: That is not my point. My point is, whether you are creative or merely listening to somebody who points out all this.

Questioner: I think you create when you observe uncritically.

KRISHNAMURTI: Not 'I think'. You see, Sir, I passionately want to find out.

Questioner: The moment you see that you are attached, in that very moment you see and act. That is the moment of creation.

KRISHNAMURTI: Therefore you are saying, seeing is acting and at that moment there is creation. That is a definition.

Questioner: Is not creativity one's harmony with Nature.

KRISHNAMURTI: Are you in harmony with nature? You miss the point. I want to find out, I am hungry, I have observed all the great painters, I have seen all the great plays and so on. I ask what is creation? What is it to be creative? Do not give a definition, I want to learn!

Questioner: Doing something new is creative.

KRISHNAMURTI: What does that mean? Something totally new and fresh, without a decision? That means the past must end. Has it ended with you? Or are you just talking about creation as you talk about a book. If you are, I don't want to play a part in it. I want to *learn,* I am passionate, I want to shed tears over it! One can live creatively without doing any of these things, neither baking bread, painting a picture, or writing a poem. You can only do that when the mind is non-fragmentary, when there is no fear, when the mind is free of all the implications of the past, when the mind is free of the known.

Questioner: For me, creativity isn't a thing, it's a movement.

KRISHNAMURTI: Not for you, Sir, nor for me — you are all making it personal. It is not an opinion. I am hungry and you feed me with a lot of words. Which means, you are not hungry. Yesterday, after talking about attachment, I was watching it; the mind was watching all day, whether it was attached to *anything,* to sitting on a platform, talking, wanting to tell people, writing something, or being attached to a person, to ideas, to a chair. One has to find out and in finding out one discovers enormous things, the beauty of freedom and the love that comes out of that freedom. When we are talking of creation, it means a mind that has no aggression.

So to find out about the machinery, the network of habit, one has to be aware, go into it, let it flow through you, like that river which is moving. Let this enquiry carry you all day and you will discover enormous things.

4th August 1970.

Dialogue 4

To see the whole network of fears and escapes. The struggle with attachment is a movement only in fragmentation. Can one arrive at completeness, enlightenment, through fragmentation? How does fragmentation arise? Thought and the category of time. Seeing thought divides and yet is a necessary function, what will you do about it? The function of the mind that is free of the known. To put the impossible question.

KRISHNAMURTI: We have been talking about attachment, which inevitably leads to fear. And we talked about the various forms of fear; both the conscious and the unconscious fear one has. We are asking whether one can see the whole network of fears and escapes without analysis but rather observe them without any analytical process at all. I think we ought to go into this matter very deeply because a mind that is not free from fear and the different forms of escape from that fear will inevitably be crippled, made unintelligent, even though it may follow various systems of meditation and so on, which is utterly childish and immature, as long as there is not complete freedom from fear.

So could we go into it much more deeply and find out and learn about the mind? Not only about the superficial layers but also penetrate the deep, hidden layers of the mind in which there are fears. As most people are attached to something or other, that attachment indicates an escape from one's own loneliness, one's own frustrations, emptiness and shallowness. Now when one is aware of this whole movement of fear — which is a movement away from the fact of emptiness — can one see this total process as a whole and not partially? That is what we are talking about.

To see something whole, the fragmentary process of the mind that seeks success must come to an end. 'I want to be free from fear in order to achieve something else', or 'I will follow certain systems of meditation in order to arrive at enlightenment'; 'I will discipline, control, shape myself in order to see something most extraordinary.' Such a way of thinking, living and acting is fragmentary. I don't know if we see all that clearly.

Can we look at the network of fear from which our whole being runs away, and the various escapes from it? Can we see these complicated, very subtle forms of escapes which are the very nature of fear? Can we see that to act from any form of conclusion is fragmentary, because it stops further learning; you may have started to learn, but the moment there is a conclusion from that learning it becomes fragmentary. What makes for fragmentation? We have discussed fear when we find ourselves attached to something and the cultivation of detachment in order to overcome fear. That is fragmentary thinking. What is it that makes for fragmentation in our life? Please Sirs, don't draw any conclusions from what you hear. I really want to communicate with you to tell you that one can become completely, totally and utterly free of fear; not only of the biological, physical fears, but of the deep down psychological fears.

Fear is a form of fragmentation. Attachment is a form of fragmentation. And seeing attachment, the attempt to be detached is a movement in fragmentation. I am attached to my family; then I discover that causes pain or pleasure. If it is painful I want to detach myself from it and fight attachment. So it is a movement in fragmentation and therefore there is no resolution in that fragmentation. What is the basis, the mechanism, of this fragmentation in life? Not only inwardly but outwardly — this breaking up into different nationalities, religions, practices? Through one of these fragments one hopes to arrive at a synthesis, at a completeness, at enlightenment — whatever you like to call it. That is, through fragmentation you hope to achieve a non-fragmentary mind. Is that possible? The yogis, the rishes and the various gurus promise all these things. So one has to find out why fragmentation comes into being, what its mechanism is. Not conclude verbally or intellectually, what the process of it is, but actually see the whole mechanism of it non-analytically. I

130

don't know if I am conveying this to you? If I am not, please let's stop and discuss it.

Questioner: These wise men, these rishes as you call them, aren't they enlightened men?

KRISHNAMURTI: What do you think? You are asking my opinion? Only fools give opinions! (*Laughter*) How do you know who is enlightened? You never ask that. I may sit on the platform and say I am the wisest, most enlightened, most divine human being, but how do you know? This is what is happening in the world. A man comes and makes these assertions, says do certain things and you will have enlightenment. 'I have got it, I will give it to you.' How do you know whether he is enlightened? Why do you bother about who is enlightened or who is not enlightened?

Questioner: You can experience yourself if you do certain things, you can have a method.

KRISHNAMURTI: No, Sir, there is no method. We are not showing you a method at all, we are learning. Learning is not a method; you can learn through a method, but it only conditions the mind to that particular system. If you are learning, you observe. If you observe that one system conditions the mind and makes it mechanical, then all systems are the same; you learn what a system does. Through some system you can have a most extraordinary experience, but it is still a very limited experience — this is so obvious.

Questioner: Couldn't it be that to start off with, you could use a system, just to get an idea of it, even if it is only partial, and then from there go on to get the big thing.

KRISHNAMURTI: Wouldn't it be helpful to begin with the

crutches and later on throw them off? Our question is, why do you hold on to any strings when you can observe, learn from watching yourself the whole phenomenon of existence and go beyond it? Sir, you want to be helped; if I may point out most respectfully that is the greatest impediment. You have the idea somebody can teach you, therefore you begin right off with a fragmentation; this division is a fragmentation — you and the teacher, you and the enlightened being — obviously there is a division.

Questioner: But aren't you teaching?

KRISHNAMURTI: Am I? From the beginning the speaker has said there is no teacher and no disciple. He has been saying this for forty-five years, not out of foolishness or as a reaction, but because he perceived the truth that nobody can teach enlightenment to another through any system, nor through meditation, nor through any discipline. One saw that forty-five years ago. And you ask: are you a teacher or not? I've shown it to you. A teacher implies one who has accumulated knowledge and transmits it to another; like a professor and a student. We are not in that relationship here at all. We are learning together, we have made that very clear. All communication means learning together, creating together, watching together. If that is understood then our communication is entirely different. But if you have a feeling that because the speaker sits on the platform he knows better, he is the enlightened one, I say: please don't attribute things to the person who is sitting on the platform. You know nothing about enlightenment. If you knew it or if you understood it, lived it, you wouldn't be here. It is one of the most extraordinary things to find out, to learn about; not 'to be taught' — you don't pay a hundred dollars to be taught this. Just to think — paying money to learn the truth! What are you all doing?

So, Sirs, we are trying to find out, to learn what is implied in fragmentation. The teacher and the disciple — that is a fragmentation. The higher self and the lower self, the soul and the body, this constant division.

Questioner: Thought is only capable of giving attention to one thing at a time. Are you saying that thought is the cause of fragmentation? If thought can only give attention to that and discard all the rest, then thought must breed fragmentation; the very process of thinking is fragmentation.

KRISHNAMURTI: We are going to learn about it — please don't draw a conclusion. I am asking why we live in fragmentation, how does it happen? And what is behind the demand for this fragmentation? Let's take a very simple fact. You are the teacher and I am the disciple; why is there this division between you and me? Do I want to learn, or do I want to follow the authority which you represent, which you have invested in yourself? You say you know, you are enlightened. And I want to have that, I am greedy, I want something that will give me happiness. So I follow you, the teacher, as the disciple; fragmentation exists when I follow you. I have never asked why I follow you. What is the reason, what is the basis of accepting you as my authority? You may be a crazy neurotic, you may have had some little experiences which you have blown up to be a tremendous thing, and I am incapable of judging because you fascinate me by your beard or your eyes, or whatever it is, and I just follow. Whereas I want to learn, I won't accept you as the authority, because the moment you become the authority you have already brought about fragmentation. Please do see that.

It doesn't matter whether it is the spiritual, or the political, or the military authority. The moment there is the assumption of authority — the assumption that you know and I don't know — there is fragmentation. And that will inevitably lead to conflict between you, the teacher, and me. Is this clear? So that means, I will *never* follow anybody.

Questioner: If he does good to you, Sir, why shouldn't you do it? Isn't it better to have something fragmentary than nothing?

KRISHNAMURTI: The teacher tells me something and I do it and in the doing of it I have great delight, great pleasure; I have understood. What is implied in that? My craving for experience, my craving to understand — not myself, but what the guru is saying. If the guru said, 'Understand yourself', that is far more important than anything else. Don't try to understand me, but understand yourself. You would rather follow than understand yourself! So why is there this fragmentation?

Questioner: Because we are made of fragmentary processes, our faculties are fragmentary. Each faculty has a partial activity.

KRISHNAMURTI: You have a faculty for engineering. Why should fragmentation arise from that faculty? I have a faculty for playing the piano. Why should that bring about a fragmentation? Aren't you putting the cart before the horse? Is it the faculty that brings about fragmentation, or is the mind broken up and using one of the fragments, one of the faculties and therefore further strengthening the division? Do you understand what I am saying?

I want to learn about this fragmentation. If I could once solve that, my action would be altogether different, it would be non-fragmentary; so I must find out. I am not going to come to any conclusion or start with any conclusion. There is fragmentation — the teacher and the disciple, the authority, the follower, the man who says he is enlightened, the man who says, 'I don't know', the Communist, the Socialist — why? How does it happen? If I could really understand it, learn all about it, I would be finished with it. Then my relationship with another will be entirely different, then my activities will be total each time. So I *must* learn about it. What do you say, Sirs?

Questioner: We live in expectation and desire.

KRISHNAMURTI: We live in expectation, and that very expectation is a form of fragmentation. What are you expecting? Is that the real reason for fragmentation? It is one of the effects of fragmentation, like wanting success. Is wanting success the effect of my fragmentation? That is tremendously important. I want success — through painting or writing, through this or that. So what is the basis of this fragmentation?

Questioner: It is because each of our faculties is limited, our view is limited, our senses and our intelligence are limited; one has not the possibility of seeing the whole at once.

KRISHNAMURTI: My view is in one direction only, if I had eyes at the back of my head I would see the whole thing. Is that what we are discussing? And saying my view is limited? Of course my physical view is limited, I can't see the whole Alpine range — perhaps I could if I went up in an aeroplane. But surely that is not what we are discussing? We are discussing why the mind, the brain, divides.

Questioner: It is not possible to think of the whole world at once.

KRISHNAMURTI: So you are saying, fragmentation exists as long as there is thought, which cannot think about the whole thing at once; that is the cause of fragmentation.

Questioner: Yes, our communication with other people is also fragmentary; right now we are thinking about self-knowledge and not about mountain climbing. You can't put everything together.

KRISHNAMURTI: Now let's be clear what we are talking about. Not climbing the mountain — as you point out, Sir — or having eyes at the back of the head. But we are talking of our mind, of our ways of thinking, looking, listening, coming to conclusions. Why is there this process which inevitably brings about fragmentation? That is what we are discussing.

Questioner: Discussing all this is already fragmentary.

KRISHNAMURTI: So discussing this very issue is a fragmentation. But we are asking why this fragmentation exists. Why can't I communicate with you completely and you convey to me completely? Let's find out, let's go into this slowly. What is the process, the mechanism, the cause of this fragmentation?

Questioner: Because we cling to our ideas about ourselves and to our ideas about certain things.

KRISHNAMURTI: Yes, we cling to a conclusion, and that is the reason of fragmentation. Why do we cling to a conclusion?

Questioner: I still think it is due to communication. For instance, at school you receive lessons in French and English and Geography. From the beginning education is fragmentary.

KRISHNAMURTI: You are saying, our education is fragmentary and therefore our mind is already conditioned from childhood by this fragmentation.

Questioner: The process of thinking is to form conclusions; you can't think without forming a conclusion.

KRISHNAMURTI: So you are all saying, in more or less different words, that thought is the source of all fragmentation.

Questioner: Thought is a fragment of ourselves.

KRISHNAMURTI: Yes, thought, which is thinking, is fragmentary. It is a fragment of ourselves.

136

Questioner: The result of all our thinking, our conclusions, must result in further fragmentation.

KRISHNAMURTI: That's right, Sir. So you are saying to me, who am learning as you are learning, that thought is the source of all fragmentation. Find out, don't say yes or no. Thought is the result, or the response of memory and memory is the past. And that memory of the past is always divided — obviously. The past, today and tomorrow; the past experience, the present experience and the future. The past that says, 'I haven't learnt, I don't know, and I am going to learn from you'. Isn't that the major cause of fragmentation? What do you say, Sirs?

Questioner: You already said so when you were speaking about time. The awareness of time is taking our attention away from the present so it divides.

KRISHNAMURTI: Time divides surely. What is time? Find out, Sir. There is chronological time: I have to go to the station to catch a train which goes at a certain time. And there is time as achievement, as success, as 'you know', 'I don't know', 'I'm going to learn'. All that involves psychological time. That is, thought says, 'I am going to learn step by step'. Gradually I am to climb all the steps and eventually come to that marvellous state; so there is a division created by thought which wants success. The success not being money this time, but enlightenment or faith.

So are you saying that thought is the mechanism that brings about this fragmentation? The thought that has said, 'You are a Hindu', 'You are a Catholic', 'You are brown', 'You are black', and 'You are pink'. Thought has conditioned the values of a particular society and culture, which says everybody who does not belong to that culture is a barbarian. This is all clear, isn't it? If thought is responsible for this fragmentation, what are you going to do about it? I have to earn a livelihood — I have to in order to live, I have a family. And also there is 'me', with my

137

problems, with my ambitions, with my successes.

So there is the livelihood, there is the family, there is the function and the desire to derive status from that functioning, and the me — all fragmented. Now what am I to do? I see thought is responsible for all this. Is that so or not? We are learning — if the speaker is wrong, tell him, find out!

Questioner: But we are thinking all the time, we are thinking at this very moment.

KRISHNAMURTI: Wait, we are going to find out. That is the whole point. We are thinking and we say, 'I have to earn a livelihood, there is the family, enjoyment, success, wanting to find enlightenment, the guru, authority, all that'. And there is me muddling through all this. And you tell me that thought is responsible for this. I have thoughts which have brought about a certain culture and that culture has conditioned me. Thought has done this and thought also has to earn a livelihood. Thought says you must earn money for your family, for your children. So thought is responsible for it. Are you sure you are right? Don't say afterwards it is not like that — be quite sure, learn.

Questioner: One has the feeling that there is something even behind thought.

KRISHNAMURTI: We'll come to that. First see what we are dealing with. But you can't come to what is behind thought without understanding the whole machinery of thought; otherwise you'll be merely escaping from thought. Now is that the truth — not your truth or my truth, not my personal opinion or your opinion — is it the fact, that thought divides? Thought divides the living now and the dying tomorrow. I will die to-morrow, but thought says, 'You'll die', 'You'll get frightened!' Or thought says, 'That was a marvellous pleasure, I must have more of it'. And thought says, 'I am frightened of what I have done, be careful, don't let it occur again, don't let it be discovered'. So thought is breeding fear, pain and pleasure. Thought divides. That is the truth, whether you see it or not. So knowing thought brings about fragmentation and therefore sustains division — what are you going to do?

Questioner: Does thought itself divide, or is it the way we use our thoughts?

KRISHNAMURTI: Who is the 'we'? Who is the 'I' that uses thought which divides?

Don't come to any conclusion, first listen to what the speaker is saying. Livelihood has to be earned, so thought must be employed there. I come back home and thought says, 'my family', 'my responsibility'. Or it says, 'I have great pleasure in sex', 'I am in great pain, my wife may run away'. Thought is in operation all the time, breeding fragmentation — the teacher, the disciple, the success. What are you going to do, knowing that thought brings about fragmentation, which means fear, which means conflict? Fragmentation means that there will be no peace whatsoever. You may talk about peace, join an organisation that promises peace, but there will be no peace as long as there is fragmentation by thought. So faced with that fact, what is going to happen?

Questioner: I identify myself with the thought.

KRISHNAMURTI: Who is the 'I' who identifies itself with thought? Has not thought created the 'I'? The 'I' being my experiences, my knowledge, my success — which is all the product of thought. And if you say it is the higher self, God, it is still thought; you have thought about God. So what will you do?

Questioner: Thought must end.

KRISHNAMURTI: How is it to end? Listen, Sir, thought must operate when you do something mechanical, even to drive a car. You say thought must end altogether. Then you can't earn a livelihood, you can't go home, you won't be able to speak. Sir, watch yourself, find out, learn about this! Thought must be used and thought also sees that it breeds fragmentation. So what is thought to do?

Questioner: It seems that we come to this point in almost every discussion. My question is: is that a question that can be answered?

KRISHNAMURTI: We're going to find out.

Questioner: I become afraid, because I see the deadlock of it.

KRISHNAMURTI: Now knowing that you don't know what to do, will you learn Sir?

Questioner: If it is possible.

KRISHNAMURTI: Why do you say 'if it is possible'? My question is not whether it is possible or not, but I said, 'Will you learn about this?' To learn — what does it imply? Curiosity — doesn't it? Don't disagree casually. Are you eager, passionate to learn about this? Because this may solve *all* our problems. Therefore you must be intense, curious, passionate to find out. Are you? Or are you going to say, 'I am going to wait, so far I have functioned with conclusions, I'll form another conclusion and act from that'.

If you want to learn, these three things are absolutely necessary: curiosity, eagerness and you must have energy; that energy gives you the passion to find out, to learn. Do you have these things? Or do you just want to talk about this casually?

Questioner: Is it one-pointedness?

KRISHNAMURTI: No Sir, learning is not one-pointed learning. Learning means to have a mind that wants to learn, that wants to find out; like a child that says, 'I want to know what the mountain is made of'.

Questioner: I may become attached to learning.

KRISHNAMURTI: Sir, why do you translate what has been said into your own words? I said one must have a great deal of energy, one must be curious to find out, and one must be persistent; not just one minute be full of curiosity and the next say, 'Sorry, I'm too tired, I'm bored, I want to go out and smoke'. Then you can't learn.

Questioner: I have a need for certainty. I am afraid if I have no certainty.

KRISHNAMURTI: Listen to that question: 'I will learn if it guarantees me complete certainty for the rest of my life'.

Questioner: This fragmentation gives me a feeling of security and I need this illusion.

KRISHNAMURTI: And you come along and disturb my security! I am therefore frightened, I don't want to learn. This is what you are all doing! I have found great delight in writing a book and I know I function from fragmentation, but that book gives me fame, money, position. Don't talk to me, the house is burning, but don't disturb me!

Let's proceed from this. If thought is the source of all fragmentation and yet thought has to be used, what is to take place? How is thought not to function and yet to function?

Thought is responsible for fragmentation and all conclusions are fragmentations. Please see that. 'I must be secure', 'I am frightened of uncertainty'. But there may be a way of living

141

which will give you physical security — which is what you want — yet psychological freedom. That freedom will bring about complete physical security, but you don't see this; so we are going to learn.

If thought is responsible for fragmentation and yet thought must function in order to survive, then what is thought to do? Do you understand my question? If you don't understand it, please let's go into this question itself. I must use thought to go from here to where I live, to earn money, to go to my job and function there properly. And yet thought itself sees that it is the cause of fragmentation and therefore conflict. Thought sees it must function, and thought sees itself bringing about fragmentation.

Questioner: Is seeing the fragmentation actually a linkage between the fragments?

KRISHNAMURTI: No Sir, it is not a linkage, you cannot put fragments together and make them a whole. The many spokes of the wheel don't make the wheel — it's how you put the spokes together that makes the wheel.

Questioner: As we have to use thought, and as we don't want fragmentation, can't we just become conscious of the tendency of thought to produce this fragmentation?

KRISHNAMURTI: If you are conscious that thought brings about fragmentation, the very consciousness of this whole process brings about a different quality altogether. Is that what you are saying? Is that what is happening to you? Be careful Sir, go very slowly into this. Thought must be exercised, and thought also realises that it breeds fragmentation and therefore conflict and fear and all the misery in the world. Yet thought itself — you are suggesting — must be conscious of this whole process. Now see what happens. We said thought is the basis of fragmentation;

142

therefore when thought becomes conscious of itself and how it breeds fragmentation, thought divides itself into this and into that.

Questioner: We must use thought and must be conscious of the sort of thought which is causing fragmentation.

KRISHNAMURTI: Go into this slowly. What do you mean by that word 'conscious'?

Questioner: To see.

KRISHNAMURTI: What do you mean by 'seeing'? Do you see this process mechanically? Because you have heard the words, you have intellectually understood, and you see with the intention of applying these words and the intellectual conclusion to seeing. Be careful, don't say 'no'. Are you seeing with a conclusion or are you merely seeing? Have you understood?

Questioner: At the point where you were asking this question, were you yourself actually asking the question? Because it seems to me, that if there is a question at this point, it is again a fragmentation.

KRISHNAMURTI: The lady suggests, if you are asking the question, then you are again beginning a fragmentation.

Questioner: And if so, what has this whole investigation been? What validity has it had?

KRISHNAMURTI: I'll explain it to you. You come to this point and ask the question. And the lady says, 'Who is asking this question?' Is it thought that is asking the question? If it is, then it is again a fragmentation. I am asking it because you are not learning. Therefore I am going to find out.

I have this picture — the mind sees that much — how thought has fragmented; thought must function and sees this. If you really see this completely, there is no more question. You can only see this if there is no conclusion, no desire to solve it, to go beyond it. Only when you see this whole mechanism of thought completely — how it operates, how it functions, what is behind all this — then the problem is solved. Then you are functioning all the time non-fragmentarily; even though you go to the office, it is a non-fragmentary action if you see the whole of it. If you don't then you divide into the office, the family, the you, the me. Now, do you see the whole of it?

Questioner: Sir, are you suggesting it is possible to carry on a non-dualistic life and still function in society?

KRISHNAMURTI: I am showing it to you, Sir, if you see this whole mechanism of thought, not just one part of it, the whole nature and structure and the movement of it.

Questioner: How can you learn it more quickly?

KRISHNAMURTI: By listening *now*! You see, again there is the desire to achieve! That means you are not listening at all; your eyes, your ears, are fixed on getting somewhere.

So, Sir, my question then is, asking as a friend, do you see this whole thing? And the friend says: 'You must see it, otherwise you're going to live a terrible, miserable existence — you'll have wars, you'll have such sorrow — for God's sake see this!' And why don't you? What is preventing you? Your ambition? Your laziness? The innumerable conclusions that you have?

Now, who is going to answer it?

Questioner (1): Why answer it? Just do *it.*
Questioner (2): I know I have conclusions, but I can't get rid of them, they go on.

144

Questioner (3): How can we ever be secure?

KRISHNAMURTI: It is the same old question. Tell me how to be secure; that is the everlasting question of man.

Questioner: Maybe it is good to become more aware that we are living now and not yesterday or last year. A lot of our attention is taken away by living in the past and dreaming of the future.

KRISHNAMURTI: Can you live in the present? Which means living a life that has no time.

Questioner: Physically, I am alive.

KRISHNAMURTI: I am asking you, Sir, can one live in the present? To live in the present there must be no time, no past, no future, no success, no ambition. Can you do it?

Questioner: Just a bit. (Laughter) The very process of building something, let's say a house, means there must be a programme.

KRISHNAMURTI: Of course, Sir. To build a house you must have an architect, the architect makes a design, and the contractor builds according to that plan. In the same way, we want a plan. You are the architect, give me the plan and I will function according to that plan.

Questioner: I wasn't saying that. I said we want to build a house which is a concrete thing to do. We must plan certain things ...

KRISHNAMURTI: So you use thought.

Questioner: So we cannot live only in the present.

KRISHNAMURTI: I never said that, Sir. When you look at this question really carefully, you will never ask, 'How am I to live in the present?'. If you see the nature and the structure of thought very clearly, then you will find that you can function from a state of mind that is always free from all thought, and yet use thought. That is real meditation, Sir, not all the phoney stuff.

Now the mind is so crowded with the known, which is the product of thought. The mind is filled with past knowledge, past experience, the whole of memory — which is part of the brain — it is filled with the known. I may translate the known in terms of the future or in terms of the present, but it is always from the known. It is this known that divides, 'knowing the past', 'I don't know', 'I shall know'. This past, with all its reservoir of memory says, 'Do this, don't do that', 'This will give you certainty, that will give you uncertainty'.

So when this whole mind, including the brain, is empty of the known, then you will use the known when it is necessary, but functioning always from the unknown — from the mind that is free of the known. Sir, *this happens,* it's not as difficult as it sounds. If you have a problem, you think about it for a day or two, you mull it over, and you get tired of it, you don't know what to do, you go to sleep. The next morning, if you are sensitive, you have found the answer. That is, you have tried to answer this problem in terms of what is beneficial, what is successful, what will bring you certainty, in terms of the known, which is thought. And after exercising every thought, thought says, 'I'm tired'. And next morning you've found the answer. That is, you have exercised the mind, used thought to its fullest extent, and dropped it. Then you see something totally new. But if you keep on exercising thought all the time, form conclusion after conclusion — which is the known — then obviously you never see anything new.

This demands a tremendous inward awareness, an inward sense of order; not disorder, but order.

Questioner: Is there not a method of procedure?

KRISHNAMURTI: Look, Sir — I get up, walk a few paces and go down the steps. Is that a method of procedure? I just get up and do it naturally, I don't invent a method first and follow it — I see it. You can't reduce everything to a method!

Questioner: Can you ever empty this storehouse of impressions which you have had?

KRISHNAMURTI: You've put a wrong question. It is a wrong question because you say 'Can you ever'. Who is the 'you' and what do you mean by 'ever'? Which means: is it possible?

Sirs, look, we never put the impossible question — we are always putting the question of what is possible. If you put an impossible question, your mind then has to find the answer in terms of the impossible — not of what is possible. All the great scientific discoveries are based on this, the impossible. It was impossible to go to the moon. But if you say, 'It is possible' then you drop it. Because it was impossible, three hundred thousand people co-operated and worked at it, night and day — they put their mind to it and went to the moon. But we never put the impossible question! The impossible question is this: can the mind empty itself of the known? — *itself*, not *you* empty the mind. That is an impossible question. If you put it with tremendous earnestness, with seriousness, with passion, you'll find out. But if you say, 'Oh, it is possible', then you are stuck.

5th August 1970.

Dialogue 5

The conscious and the unconscious; what are the frontiers of consciousness? Is this division real, or part of fragmentation? Who 'wants to know' about the unconscious? Neurosis as an exaggeration of fragmentation. The need to see the futility of identification with the fragment; a fragment as 'the observer'. 'Becoming' and 'being something' is the consciousness in which we live: a way of resistance. The difference between seeing this as an observation, and seeing that 'this is the "me"'. Dreams. Is one in a position to ask the next question: 'What is beyond consciousness'?

KRISHNAMURTI: We are going to talk over together this morning what lies below the conscious. I do not know if you have enquired into it at all, or have merely accepted what the analysts and the psychologists have said. But if you go into it fairly deeply — as I hope we shall this morning — one or two major fundamental questions have to be asked. One has to discover, explore, learn for oneself, the whole content of consciousness. Why does one divide the unconscious and the conscious? Is it an artificial division brought about by the analysts, the psychologists, the philosophers? Is there a division at all? If one is to enquire into the whole structure and the nature of consciousness, who is it that is going to enquire? A fragment of the many fragments? Or is there an entity, an agency, that is beyond all this which looks into consciousness? Can the conscious mind, the daily operative mind, observe the contents of the unconscious or deeper layers? And what are the frontiers of consciousness? What are the limits?

This is a very serious subject. I think in the understanding of it most human problems will be resolved. It isn't a thing that you take up as a hobby to study for a couple of weeks superficially and then drop it to go on with your daily life. If one is to go into this deeply, it is a way of life. It is not that you understand *that* and leave it there. You can only understand the whole content of consciousness and the limits of consciousness if it is a daily concern. It isn't a thing you can play with. It must be your whole life, your whole calling, your vocation. Because we are enquiring into the very depths of the human mind, not according to your opinion, or the speaker's opinion, but learning the fullness of it and seeing what lies beyond it — not just scratching the surface and thinking you have understood it. It isn't a thing that you learn from a book, or from another. Please do let us realise this: it isn't a thing that you acquire as knowledge from books and then apply it. If you do that it will have no value, it will be second-hand. And if you merely treat it as a form of intellectual, spiritual or emotional entertainment, then equally it will have no effect at all in your life. We are concerned with the fundamental revolution of the mind, of the whole structure of oneself — for the mind to free itself of all its conditioning. So that we are not just educated and sophisticated, but real, mature, deep human beings.

This morning we are going to learn together, if we can, what is below the conscious, and seeing the many layers (or the one layer) to discover for ourselves the content of consciousness: whether that content makes up the conscious, or whether the conscious with its frontier contains 'what is'. Does the content of consciousness make up consciousness? Do you follow? Or do all these things exist in the content? Do you see the difference? I am just investigating, I am moving slowly, so let us travel together. Don't ask me afterwards 'Please repeat what you said' — I can't.

First, why is there this division between the conscious and the so-called unconscious or the deeper layers? Are you aware of this division? Or does this division exist because we have got so many divisions in our life? Which is it? Is the conscious movement a separate movement and have the deeper layers their own movement, or is this whole thing an undivided movement? This is very important for us to find out, because we have trained the conscious mind, we have drilled it, educated it, forced it, shaped it, according to the demands of society and according to our own impulses, our own aggression and so on. Is the unconscious, the deeper layer, uneducated? We have educated the superficial layers; are we educating the deeper layer? Or are the deeper layers utterly untouched. What do you say?

In the deeper layers there may be the source and means of finding out new things, because the superficial layers have become mechanical, they are conditioned, repetitive, imitative; there is no freedom to find out, to move, to fly, to take to the wind! And in the deeper layers, which are not educated, which are unsophisticated and therefore extraordinarily primitive — primitive, not savage — there may be the source of something new.

I do not know what you feel, what you have discovered. Is the superficial mind so heavily conditioned that it has become mechanical? If I am a Hindu or Christian I function as a Hindu or Christian, or whatever it is. And below that, is there a layer which education has not touched? Or has it, and therefore the whole content of consciousness is mechanical? Are you following?

Questioner: Sir, how can we know about the unconscious?

KRISHNAMURTI: All right Sir, let's begin. When we use the word 'know', what do we mean by that? I am not being merely verbal, but we must move into this very carefully. What do you mean when you say, 'I want to know'?

Questioner: I haven't any experience of it.

KRISHNAMURTI: Keep to that one word, go into it, don't introduce other words. What do you mean by that word 'know'? When you use that word, what does it mean? 'I know something that has happened yesterday.' All knowledge is the past — isn't it? Don't agree please, just see. I know you because I met you yesterday. I didn't meet the whole of you, I only met you when you were saying something; therefore knowing implies within a certain period of time. So knowledge always implies the past. When I say, 'I know that is an aeroplane flying', though the flying is taking place at this moment, the knowledge that it is an aeroplane is of the past. How can the superficial mind learn about the deeper layers? How can that superficial mind learn about the other?

Questioner: Keep the superficial mind still, then it can learn about the deeper levels.

KRISHNAMURTI: What is there to learn in the deeper layers? You assume there is something to learn; are you actually aware of the operations of the conscious mind? How it is ticking over? What its responses are? Is there an awareness of the conscious mind? Find out how extraordinarily difficult this is. The mind has to watch this entire movement very closely. You say in the unconscious there are many things. That's what all the professionals say — are there? The moment you divide the conscious from the deeper layers, the question arises: how is this superficial mind to enquire into the other? If there is no division at all, it is a total movement in which one is only aware of a fragmentary movement. This fragmentary movement asks: what are the contents of the unconscious? If it is a total movement you won't ask this question. Is the speaker making this clear? Be quite sure, not verbally but actually.

The moment you divide consciousness into fragments, one fragment says: 'what are the other fragments?' But if it is a total movement then there is no fragmentation, therefore the question doesn't arise. This is really important to find out about. Then you go beyond all the specialists. Do you see consciousness as a whole, or do you see with one fragment which examines the other fragments? Do you see it partially, or wholly as a total movement, like a river that is moving? You can dig a ditch along the bank and call it the river — it isn't. In the river there

151

is the whole movement. Then what is this movement? How is one to observe without fragmentation?

Questioner: May I say something please? You speak about an unconscious mind. But is there an unconscious mind? You cannot speak about something which is not. But we can speak about the conscious. Please define conscious and unconscious. The question is: are we now unconscious?

KRISHNAMURTI: We asked this question earlier: are we aware of the frontiers of consciousness? Or are we aware of the many fragments that compose the conscious? Does one fragment become aware of the many other fragments? Or are you aware of the total movement of consciousness without any division?

Questioner: Both ways are conscious. Intellectually we are dividing ourselves into parts.

KRISHNAMURTI: Please see we are not analysing. Where there is analysis there is the analyser and the thing analysed — one fragment assuming the authority of analysis and examining the other part. And in this division arise the conscious and the unconscious. Then we put the question: can the conscious mind examine the unconscious? — which implies that the conscious mind is separate from the rest. We say that from this false question you can answer this through dreams, through various forms of intimations and hints. All arising from a false assumption that the superficial mind is separate from the other; which means we have never seen or felt or learnt about the movement of conciousness as a whole. If you do, this question doesn't arise at all. I don't know if you see this?

Questioner: Obviously some people are suffering from neurosis without knowing the origin of it. Isn't that in the unconscious?

KRISHNAMURTI: Do you suffer from a neurosis? Please, this is not a silly question. Are you aware that you are neurotic in some form or another?

152

Questioner: Who decides if one is neurotic?

KRISHNAMURTI: Don't you know when you are neurotic? Has somebody got to tell you that you are neurotic? Do please listen to this. When there is any exaggeration of any fragment then neurosis takes place. When you are highly intellectual that is a form of neurosis, though the highly intellectual is greatly regarded. Holding on to certain beliefs, Christian, Buddhist, Communist, attachment to any belief, is a form of neurosis. Sir, look at it, go slowly. Hold on to your question. Any fear is a form of neurosis, any conformity is a form of neurosis, and any form of comparing yourself with something else is neurotic. Aren't you doing all this?

Questioner: Yes.

KRISHNAMURTI: Therefore you are neurotic! (*Laughter*) No, no, please Sir, this is very serious. We have learned something from this. Any exaggeration of any fragment of the whole consciousness as we see it — which contains many fragments — any emphasis on any fragment is a form of neurosis. Sirs, get it into your hearts, feel it, move, take time, get involved in it, apply it to yourself, and you will see the next question.

As we are, we have divided consciousness; in this division there are many fragmentations, many divisions: the intellectual, emotional and so on; and any emphasis on that division is neurotic. Which means that a mind emphasising a fragment cannot see clearly. Therefore the emphasis of a fragment brings about confusion. I am asking you to see for yourself whether there is not a fragmentation in you; that fragmentation laying emphasis on one thing, on its issues, on its problems, and disregarding the other fragments, leads not only to conflict but to great confusion, because each fragment demands an expression, each demands an emphasis, and when you emphasise the one the others are clamouring. This clamour is confusion and out of that confusion come neurotic impulses, all forms of desire to fulfil, to become, to achieve.

Questioner: Sometimes what you suffer from is not the apparent thing. If somebody doesn't dare to cross a square, it is obviously not the square he is frightened of. Or if one is afraid to be alone, it may be something in the unconscious which causes the fear.

KRISHNAMURTI: Yes. The neurosis is only a symptom, the cause could be in the unconscious. Obviously this could be so and probably is. Then what is the question?

Questioner: It's a neurosis.

KRISHNAMURTI: When we have understood this whole structure, then we can go into the particular; but to start with the particular will lead nowhere. Do you see that any emphasis on the fragment is a form of neurosis? There is the intellectual, the emotional, the physical, the psychosomatic; most of us have laid stress on one aspect of the many fragments. Out of that exaggeration, out of that disharmony, other factors of disharmony arise. Such as: 'I can't cross a street', or 'I am frightened in the dark'; and the explanation is that in my childhood my mother didn't treat me properly!

Now our question is not why I can't cross the street, which I shall answer without going to the analyst, if I understand the fragmentation of consciousness. The moment I have understood that, then the problem of crossing the street doesn't exist at all. Are we meeting each other? When we see the greater, the totality, the immensity, the lesser disappears. But if we keep on emphasising the little, then the little brings about its own little problems.

Questioner: But when you talk about seeing the totality of consciousness, what does 'seeing' mean? For instance, sometimes I know something but I don't know how I know it.

KRISHNAMURTI: No Sir, just look. Do you listen to the movement of that river totally? Just *do* it Sir. Don't speculate. Listen to that river and find out if you are listening completely, without any movement in any direction. Then after having listened, what do you say?

Questioner: Recognition plays no part in it.

KRISHNAMURTI: That's right. Recognition plays no part in it. You don't say, 'That is the stream to which I am listening'; nor are you as an entity listening to the stream; there is only the listening to the sound. You don't say, 'I know it is a river'. So let's go back. I want to go into this so much, please, let's move together.

Questioner: Is the emphasis on fragmentation the essence of neurosis, or is it the symptom?

KRISHNAMURTI: It is the very essence *and* the symptom.

Questioner: Being intellectual is the essence as well as the symptom?

KRISHNAMURTI: Isn't it? Look Sir. I emphasise my intellectual capacity. I think it is marvellous, I can beat everybody at an argument, I have read so much, I can correlate all that I have read, and I write wonderfully clever books. Isn't that the very cause and the symptom of my neurosis?

Questioner: It seems to be a symptom of our deeper disturbance.

KRISHNAMURTI: Is it? You are saying that is a symptom, not the cause. I say, let's look. Is the mind whole, undivided, and therefore are the cause and the effect the same? See it, Sir. What was the cause becomes the effect, and the effect becomes the cause of the next movement; there is no definite demarcation between cause and effect. What was cause yesterday has become the effect, and the effect of today becomes the cause tomorrow. It is a movement, it is a chain.

Questioner: But isn't it essential to see this whole process, rather than just cause and effect?

155

KRISHNAMURTI: That's what we are doing and that is not possible if you emphasise the intellectual, the emotional, the physical, the spiritual, and so on.

So my question, which was the first question, is: why have we divided the mind? Is it artificial, or necessary? Is it just the invention of the specialist to which we have become slaves, which we have accepted, as we accept most things so easily? We say, 'Great people say this' and we swallow it and repeat it. But when we see the fragmentation and the emphasis on this fragmentation; and when we see out of that arises the whole cause-effect chain and that it is a form of neurosis, then the mind sees the totality of the movement without division. Well Sir, do you see it?

Questioner: When there is no identification with the fragment.

KRISHNAMURTI: Yes. If you identify yourself with any one of the fragments, obviously it is the same process. That is, the process of being identified with the one, and disregarding the rest, is a form of neurosis, a contradiction. Now put the next question. Can you identify yourself with the rest of the fragments? You, a fragment, identifying with the many other fragments. Do you see the tricks we are playing with this question of identification?

Questioner: I can only say that after the identification with one fragment; because then I feel that I am incomplete . . .

KRISHNAMURTI: That's right. You feel you are incomplete, therefore you try to identify yourself with many other fragments. Now who is the entity that is trying to identify itself with the many? It is one of the fragments, therefore it is a trick — you follow? And we are doing this all the time: 'I must identify myself'.

Questioner: Isn't it better to identify yourself with many fragments so that you are more complete?

KRISHNAMURTI: No, not better. Look Sir, first let me explain

156

it again. There are many fragments of which I am. One of the fragments says it brings about confusion to identify myself with a single fragment. So it says: 'I'll identify myself with the many other fragments'. And it makes a tremendous effort to identify itself with the many fragments. Who is this entity that tries to identify itself with the other fragments? It is also a fragment, isn't it? Therefore it is only playing a game by itself. This is so simple! Now let's proceed, there is so much in this, we are just remaining on the very surface of it all.

We see there is no actual division at all. I see it non-verbally. I feel it that the observer is a fragment which separates itself from the rest of the fragments and is observing. In that observation there is a division, as the observer and the observed, there is conflict, there is confusion. When the mind realises this fragmentation and the futility of separating itself, then it sees the movement as a whole. If you cannot do this you cannot possibly put the next question, which is: what is beyond the conscious? What is below, above, beside? — it doesn't matter how you put it.

So if you are serious, you have to find out what consciousness is and when you are aware that you are conscious. Do you understand my question? I am doing all the work! Sir, look, you have to learn about all this and when you learn you help others to learn. So learn *now,* for God's sake! That is your vocation. We are asking what is this thing called consciousness? When do you say, 'I am conscious?'

Questioner: When there is thought.

KRISHNAMURTI: Come nearer.

Questioner: When there is duality.

KRISHNAMURTI: What do you mean? Come closer. You begin too far away.

Questioner: When you are in fragmentation.

157

KRISHNAMURTI: Sir, just listen. When are you at all aware that you are conscious? Is this so very difficult?

Questioner: When I am in pain.

KRISHNAMURTI: The lady suggests you are conscious when there is pain, when there is conflict, when you have a problem, when you are resisting; otherwise you are flowing smoothly, evenly, harmoniously. Living without any contradiction, are you conscious at all? Are you conscious when you are supremely happy?

Questioner: Yes.

KRISHNAMURTI: Yes?

Questioner: What does that word 'being conscious' mean?

KRISHNAMURTI: You don't have to ask me, you'll find out. The moment you are conscious that you are happy, is happiness there? The moment you say, 'How joyous I am', it has already moved away from you. Can you ever say that?

Questioner: You are then conscious of that.

KRISHNAMURTI: Which is the past! So you are only conscious of something that has happened, or when there is some conflict, some pain, when there is the actual awareness that you are confused. Any disturbance in this movement is to be conscious and all our life is a disturbance against which we are resisting. If there were no discord at all in life would you say, 'I am conscious'? When you are walking, moving, living without any friction, without any resistance, without any battle, you don't say 'I am'. It is only when you say, 'I will become' or 'I am being', then you are conscious.

Questioner: Isn't this state that you are talking about still a process of identification with the tree . . .

KRISHNAMURTI: No Sir. I explained identification. When I see a tree I don't mistake it for a woman or for the church: it is a tree. Which doesn't mean identification. Look Sir, we have

158

discovered something, we have learned something. There is consciousness only when there is 'becoming', or trying 'to be something'. Becoming implies conflict: 'I will be'. Which means conflict exists as long as the mind is caught in the verb 'to be' — please see that. Our whole culture is based on that word 'to be'. 'I will be a success', 'I am a failure', 'I must achieve', 'This book is mine, it is going to change the world'. You follow? So as long as there is a movement of becoming, there is conflict and that conflict makes the mind aware that it is conscious. Or the mind says, 'I must *be* good' — not 'I will be good'. To *be* good. Also it is a form of resistance: being good. Being and becoming are the same.

Questioner: Can one be conscious of conflict?

KRISHNAMURTI: Of course Sir, otherwise you wouldn't be conscious.

Questioner: Can't you be so caught up in conflict that you don't see that you are in conflict?

KRISHNAMURTI: Of course, it is a form of neurosis. Sir, look. Have you ever been to a mental hospital, any of you? I wasn't there as a patient, I was taken by an analyst, and all the patients from the top floor, where the most violent ones are caged in, down to the lowest floor where they are more or less peaceful, they are all in conflict — an exaggerated conflict — do you understand? Only they are inside the building and we are outside — that's all.

Questioner: I am trying to distinguish between consciousness and awareness.

KRISHNAMURTI: Both are the same. Being aware implies awareness of division. To be aware without division and choice is not to be caught in the movement of becoming or being. Have you understood? The whole movement of consciousness is either to become or to be: becoming famous, becoming a social worker, helping the world. After looking at the fragmentation, after looking at the movement of consciousness as a whole, you find that this whole movement is based on that: 'to become', or 'to be'. You have learned it, Sir — not by agreeing with me.

Then you ask a totally different question, which is: what is beyond this movement of 'becoming' and 'to be'? You are not asking that question. But I am asking it. Do you understand my question Sir? Looking at this problem of consciousness, both from the analytical and the philosophical point of view, I have realised that division has been created through 'becoming', or 'to be'. I want to be a Hindu, because it promises me not only outward success but also spiritual achievements. If I reject that, I say I must 'be' something else: I am going 'to be myself', identify myself with myself. Again this is the same process. So I observe, I see that the total movement of consciousness is this movement of being something, or becoming, or 'not to be', or 'not to become'. Now how do I see this? Do I see it as something outside myself, or do I see it without the centre, as the 'me', which observes the 'becoming' and the 'not becoming'? Have you understood my question? No, I don't think so.

I realise that all consciousness is this movement. When I say 'I realise it', am I realising it as something that I have seen outside of me, like looking at a picture hanging on the wall, spread out before me; or do I see this movement as part of me, as the very essence of me? Do I see this movement from a centre? Or do I see it without the centre? If I see it from a centre, that centre is the self, the 'me', who is the very essence of fragmentation. Therefore when there is an observation from the centre, I am only observing this movement as a fragment, as something outside of me, which I must understand, which I must try to grasp, which I must struggle with and all the rest. But if there is no centre, which means there is no 'me', but merely an observing of this whole movement, then that observation will lead to the next question. So which is it you are doing?

Please this is not group therapy, this is not a weekend entertainment, this isn't a thing you go to learn from somebody, like 'how to become sensitive', or 'how to learn creative living'; put all that aside. This is hard work, this needs deep enquiry. Now, how are you observing? If you don't understand this, life becomes a torture, a battlefield. In that battlefield you want to improve the cannon, you want to bring about brotherhood and yet keep to your isolation. We have played that game for so long! Therefore you have to answer this question if you are really profoundly serious. Are you watching this whole movement of consciousness, as we have seen it, as an outsider, unrelated to that which he is watching? Or is there no centre at all from which you are watching? And when you watch that way, what takes place?

May we sidestep a little? All of you dream a great deal, don't you? Have you ever asked why? Not how to interpret dreams, that is an irrelevant question which we'll answer presently. But have you ever asked a relevant question, which is: why do we dream at all?

Questioner: Because we are in conflict.

KRISHNAMURTI: No Sir, don't be so quick. Look at it. Why do you dream? The next question is: is there a sleep without any dream at all? Don't say 'Yes', Sir.

You all dream; what are those dreams, why do you dream? Dreams, as we said the other day, are the continuing movement of the daily activity, symbolised, put into various categories, but it is the same movement. Isn't that so? Don't agree or disagree, find out! It is so obvious. If dreams are a continuing movement of the daily action, then what happens to the brain if there is constant activity, constant chattering?

Questioner: It never rests.

KRISHNAMURTI: What happens to it?

Questioner: It gets exhausted. It wears out.

KRISHNAMURTI: It wears itself out, there is no rest, there is no seeing of anything new. The brain doesn't make itself young. All these things are implied when there is a continuous movement of daily activity, which goes on in the brain during sleep. You may foretell what might happen in the future, because while you sleep there is a little more sensitivity, a little more perception and so on; but it is the same movement. Now, can this movement, which goes on during the day, end with the day? Not be carried over when you sleep? That is, when you go to bed the whole thing is ended. Don't answer my question yet. We are going to go into it.

Doesn't it happen to you when you go to bed, that you take stock of what you have done during the day? Or do you just flop into bed and go to sleep? Don't you review the day and say, this should have been done, this should not have been done? And ask yourself the meaning of this or that? Follow this very carefully. You are bringing order. The brain demands order, because otherwise it can't function efficiently. If you dream, if the movement of the daily activity goes on in your sleep, there is no order. As the brain demands order, the brain instinctively brings about order while you are asleep. You wake up a little fresher because you have a little more order. The brain cannot function efficiently if there is any form of conflict, any form of disorder.

Questioner: Aren't there other kinds of dreams in which communications of a different kind are transmitted?

KRISHNAMURTI: First listen to this. Understand order. The movement of daily life continues through sleep because in this daily movement there is contradiction, there is disorder, disharmony. And during sleep, through dreams, through various forms of non-dreams, the brain tries to bring order into its own chaos. If you make order during the day, the brain does not need to put things in order during sleep. See the importance of this. Therefore the brain becomes rested, quiet, alive, fresh. I do not

162

know if you have noticed that when you have a problem and you go on thinking it out during the day, and it is still going on during the night, you worry about it and you wake up the next morning weary of the problem; and during the next day you still worry about that problem, like a dog biting a bone. You are at it all day and still when you go to bed again; until the brain is exhausted. Then perhaps in that exhaustion you see something fresh.

What we are saying is something entirely different. It is this: to end the problem as it arises, not to carry it over to the next day or to the next minute — end it! Somebody has insulted you, hurt you — end it! Somebody has deceived you, somebody has said unkind things about you. Look at it, don't carry it over, don't bear it as a burden. End it as it is being said, not afterwards.

Disorder is a neurotic state of the brain and ends up by producing a mental case. Order implies the ending of the problem as it arises, and therefore the movement of the daytime through the night ends and there are no dreams, because you have solved everything as you are moving. I don't know if you see the importance of this. Because then you can ask the next question, which is: what is beyond all this? We will deal with that tomorrow.

7th August 1970.

Any action out of fragmentary consciousness produces confusion.
Does the content control the structure of consciousness, or is it
free of its content? Can consciousness empty itself of its content?
The frog in the muddy pool of consciousness trying to get out.
The monkey in the space limited by the centre: self-centred
activity. What is space without a centre? 'Enlightenment ... is
that quality of mind in which the monkey never operates'.
Attention. The problem of attention and the interruptions of
the monkey. With the apogee of attention, what happens to the
whole structure of the human being?

KRISHNAMURTI: We'll go on where we left off yesterday when
we were considering the nature and the structure of consciousness. One realizes that if there is to be a radical change in the
human mind, and therefore in society, we have to consider this
question. We have to delve deeply into it to find out whether
there is a possibility of this consciousness undergoing a meta-
morphosis, a complete change in itself. Because one can see that
all our actions, superficial or profound, serious or flippant, are
the outcome of, or born out of this consciousness. And we were
saying within this consciousness there are many fragments; each
fragment assuming dominance at one time or another. If one
does not understand the content of consciousness — and the
possibility of going beyond it — any action, however significant
it may be, must produce confusion without the understanding of
the fragmentary nature of our consciousness. I think this must
be very clear. It's like giving a great deal of attention to one
fragment, like the intellect, or a belief, or the body, and so on.
These fragmentations, which compose our consciousness, from
which all action takes place, must inevitably bring about contradiction and misery. Is this clear at least verbally? To say to oneself, all these fragments must be put together or integrated has
no meaning, because then the problem arises of who is to inte-
grate them, and the effort of integration. So there must be a

way of looking at this whole fragmentation with a mind that is not fragmented. And that is what we are going to discuss this morning.

I realise that my mind, including the brain, all the physiological nervous responses, the whole of that consciousness is fragmentary, is broken up, conditioned by the culture in which one lives. That culture has been created by past generations and the coming generation. And *any* action, or the emphasis on one fragment over the others, will inevitably bring about immense confusion. Giving emphasis to social activity, to a religious belief, or intellectual concept, or Utopia, must inevitably be contradictory and therefore bring about confusion. Do we see this?

So one asks the question: is there an action which is not fragmentary and which does not contradict another action which is going to take place in the next minute?'

We see that thought plays an extraordinary part in this consciousness. Thought being not only the response of the past, but of all our feeling, all our neurological responses, the future hopes, fears, pleasures, sorrows — they are all in this. So does the content of consciousness make for the structure of consciousness? Or is consciousness free from its content?

If consciousness is made up of my despair, my anxiety, fears, pleasures, the innumerable hopes, guilts and the vast experience of the past, then any action springing from that consciousness can never free this consciousness from its limitations. Don't agree with this, it isn't just school-boy stuff! Please share it with me — which means work, observe it in yourself — and then we can proceed further. I'm just talking as an introduction.

My consciousness is the result of the culture in which I have lived. That culture has encouraged, and discouraged various activities, various pursuits of pleasure, fear, hopes and beliefs — that consciousness is the 'me'. Any action springing from that consciousness which is conditioned, must inevitably be fragmentary and therefore contradictory, confusing. If you are born in a Communist or a Socialist or a Catholic world, the culture in which that particular mind — brain — is born, is conditioned by this culture, by the standards, the values, the aspirations of that society. And any action born from this consciousness must inevitably be fragmentary. Don't ask me any questions yet — just watch yourself. First listen to what the speaker has to say, don't bring in your questions or your thoughts. Then after having listened very quietly, then you can begin to put questions, then you can say, 'You're wrong, you're right', and so on. But if that questioning is going on in your mind, then you are not listening. Therefore our communication comes to an end, we are not sharing together, and as the thing into which we are enquiring is a very complex, subtle problem, you first have to listen.

We are trying to find out what is consciousness. Is it made up of the many things that it contains, or is it something free of its content? If it is free of its content, then the action of that freedom is not dictated by the content. If it is not free, then the content dictates all action; that is simple. Now we're going to learn about it.

I realise, watching in myself, that I am the result of the past, the present, the hopes of the future. The whole throbbing quality of consciousness is all this, with all its fragmentations. Any action born of this content must inevitably be not only fragmentary, but through that there is no freedom whatsoever.

So can this consciousness empty itself and find out if there is a consciousness which is free, from which a totally different kind of action takes place? Am I conveying to you what I am talking about?

All the content of consciousness is like a shallow, muddy little pool, and a little frog is making an awful noise in it. That little frog says: 'I'm going to find out'. And that little frog is trying to go beyond itself. But it is still a frog in the muddy pool. Can this muddy pool empty all the content of itself? My little muddy pool is the culture in which I have lived and the little 'me', the frog, is battling against the culture, saying 'I must get out'. But even if it gets out, it is a little frog and whatever it gets out into, is still a little muddy pool which it will create. Please see this. The mind realises that all the activity it indulges in, or is forced into, is the movement within the consciousness with its content. Realising this, what is the mind to do? Can it ever go beyond this limited consciousness? That is one point.

The second point is: this little pool with the little frog may expand and widen. The space it creates is still within the borders of a certain dimension. That little frog — or better, that little monkey — can acquire a great deal of knowledge, information and experience. This knowledge and experience may give it a certain space to expand; but that space has always the little monkey at its centre.

So the space in consciousness is always limited by the centre. If you have a centre, the circumference of consciousness, or the frontier of consciousness, is always limited, however it may expand. The little monkey may meditate, may follow many systems, but that monkey will always remain; and therefore the space it will create for itself will always be limited and shallow. That is the second question.

The third is: what is space without a centre? We are going to find this out.

Questioner: Can this consciousness with its limitations go beyond itself?

KRISHNAMURTI: Can the monkey with all its intentions and aspirations, with all its vitality, free itself from its conditioning and go beyond the frontiers of consciousness which it has created?

To put it differently, can the 'me', which is the monkey, by doing all kinds of things — meditating, suppressing, conforming, or not conforming — being everlastingly active, can its movement take it beyond itself. That is, does the content of consciousness allow the 'me' — and therefore the attempt on the part of

167

the monkey — to free itself from the limitation of the pool? So my question is: can the monkey be completely quiet to see the extent of its own frontiers? And is it at all possible to go beyond them?

Questioner: At the centre there is always the monkey, so there is not empty space, no space for freedom.

KRISHNAMURTI: Sir, do you notice for yourself that you are always acting from a centre? The centre may be a motive, the centre may be fear, may be ambition — you are always acting from a centre, aren't you? 'I love you', 'I hate you', 'I want to be powerful' — all action as we know it, is from a centre. Whether that centre identifies with the community or with a philosophy, it is still the centre; the thing identified with becomes the centre. Are you aware of this action always going on, or are there moments when the centre is not active? It happens — suddenly you are looking, living, feeling without a centre. And that is a totally different dimension. Then thought begins to say, 'What a marvellous thing that was, I'd like to continue with it?' Then *that* becomes the centre. The remembrance of something which happened a few seconds ago becomes the centre through thought. Are we aware of the space that centre creates round itself? — the isolation, resistance, escapes. As long as there is a centre, there is the space which the centre has created and we want to expand this space, because we feel the expansion of space is necessary to live extensively. But in that expansive consciousness there is always the centre, therefore the space is always limited, however expanded. Observe it in yourself, don't listen to me, watch it in yourself, you will discover these things very simply. And the battle in relationship is between two centres: each centre wanting to expand, assert, dominate — the monkeys at work!

So I want to learn about this. The mind says, 'I see that very clearly'; the mind is learning. How does that centre come into

168

being? Is it the result of the society, the culture, or is it a divine centre — forgive me for using that word 'divine' — which has always been covered up by society, by the culture? The Hindus and others call it the Atman, the Great Thing inside which is always being smothered. Therefore you have to free the mind from being smothered, so that the real thing, the real monkey can come out.

Obviously the centre is created by the culture one lives in, by one's own conditioned memories and experiences, by the fragmentation of oneself. So it is not only the society which creates the centre, but also the centre is propelling itself. Can this centre go beyond the frontiers which it has created? By silencing itself, by controlling itself, by meditating, by following someone, can that centre explode and go beyond? Obviously it can't. The more it conforms to the pattern, the stronger it gets, though it imagines that it is becoming free. Enlightenment, surely, is that state, that quality of mind in which the monkey never operates. How is the monkey to end these activities? Not through imitation, not through conformity, not through saying, 'Somebody has attained enlightenment, I'll go and learn from him' — all those are monkey tricks.

Does the monkey see the tricks it plays upon itself by saying, 'I'm ready to help, to alter society, I am concerned with social values and righteous behaviour and social justice'. You answer this, Sir! Don't you think it is a trick that it plays upon itself? It is so clear, there is no question about it. If you're not sure, Sir, please let's discuss, let's talk it over.

Questioner: You talk sometimes as if helping society, doing social service, was something done for somebody else. But I have the feeling that I'm not different from society, so working in social service is working for myself; it's the same thing, I don't make a distinction.

KRISHNAMURTI: But if you don't make the distinction — I'm

not being personal, Sir — I'm asking, does the centre remain?

Questioner: It should not.

KRISHNAMURTI: Not 'should not'. Then we enter into quite a different field — 'should, should not, must, must not' — then it becomes theoretical. The actual fact is, though I recognise that 'me' and society are one, is the centre, the 'me', the monkey, still operating?

My question is: I see that as long as there is any movement on the part of the monkey, that movement must lead to some kind of fragmentation, illusion and chaos. To put it much more simply: that centre is the self, it is the selfishness that is always operating; whether I am godly, whether I am concerned with society and say, 'I am society' — is that centre operating? If it is, then it is meaningless.

The next question is: how is that centre to fade away? Through determination, through will, through practice, through various forms of neurotic compulsion, dedication, identification? All such movement is still part of the monkey, therefore, consciousness is within the reach of the monkey and the space within that consciousness is still within arm's length of the monkey. Therefore there is no freedom.

So the mind says, 'I see this very clearly' — 'seeing' in the sense of a perception, like seeing the microphone, without any condemnation, just seeing it. Then what takes place? To see, to listen to anything, there must be complete attention, mustn't there? If I want to understand what you are saying, I must give all my attention to it. In that attention is the monkey operative? Please find out.

I want to listen to you. You are saying something important, or unimportant, and to find out what you are saying, I must give my attention, which means my mind, my heart, my body, my nerves, everything must be in harmony to attend. The mind is not separate from the body, the heart is not separate from the mind and so on; it must be a complete harmonious whole that is attentive. That is attention. Does the mind attend with such complete attention to the activity of the monkey? — not condemning it, not saying 'This is right or wrong', just watching the tricks of the monkey. In this watching there is no analysis. This is really important Sirs, put your teeth into it! The moment it analyses one of the fragments, the monkey is in operation. So does the mind watch in this way, with such complete attention to all the movements of the monkey? What takes place when there is such *complete* attention? Are you doing it?

Do you know what it means to attend? When you are listening completely to that rain, there is no resistance against it, there is no impatience. Now when you are so listening, is there a centre with the monkey operating? Find out, Sir, don't wait for me to tell you — find out! Are you listening to the speaker with *complete* attention? Which means, not interpreting what he is saying, not agreeing or disagreeing, not comparing or translating what he is saying to suit your own particular mind; when any such activity takes place there is no attention. To attend completely means the mind is completely still to listen. Are you doing that? Are you listening to the speaker now with that attention? If you are, is there a centre there?

Questioner: We are passive.

KRISHNAMURTI: I don't care whether you are passive or active. I said, Sir, are you listening? Listening means being attentive. And in that attention is the monkey working? Don't say yes or no — find out, learn about it. And what is the quality of that attention in which there is no centre, in which the monkey isn't playing tricks?

Questioner: Is it thoughtless?

KRISHNAMURTI: I don't know, Sir, don't put it into words like 'thoughtless', 'empty'. Find out, learn, which means sustained attention — not a fleeting attention — to find out the quality of the mind that is so completely attentive.

Questioner: The moment you say the mind is not there, it is there.

KRISHNAMURTI: No, Sir — when you say it is not there to communicate through words, then the memory is there. But I am asking: when you are so completely attentive, is there a centre? Sir, surely this is simple!

When you are watching something that is really amusing and makes you laugh, is there a centre? If there is something that interests you, and if you are not taking sides and are just watching, in that watching is there a centre, which is the monkey? If there is no centre, then the question is, can this attention flow, move — not just one moment and then become inattentive — but flow naturally, easily, without effort? Effort implies the monkey coming into being. Do you follow all this?

The monkey has to come in if there is some functional work to be done. But does that operation on the part of the monkey spring from attention, or is that monkey separate from attention? Going to the office and working in the office, is that a movement of attention, or is it the movement of the monkey which has taken over, the monkey who says, 'I must be better than the others, I must make more money, I must work harder, I must compete, I must become the manager' — whatever it is. Go into it, Sir. Which is it in your life? A movement of attention, and therefore much more efficient, much more alive; or is the monkey taking over? Answer it Sir, for yourself. If the monkey takes over and makes some kind of mischief — and monkeys do make mischief — can that mischief be wiped away and not leave a mark? Go on, Sirs, you don't see the beauty of all this!

Yesterday somebody said something to me which was not

true. Did the monkey come into operation and want to say, 'You're a liar'? Or was it the movement of that attention in which the monkey is not operating? — then that statement which is not true doesn't leave a mark. When the monkey responds, then it leaves a mark. So I am asking: can this attention flow? Not, 'how can I have continuous attention', because then it is the monkey who is asking. But when there is a movement of attention all the time, the mind just moves with it.

You must answer this; it is really an extraordinarily important question. We only know the movement of the monkey and only occasionally do we have this attention in which the monkey doesn't appear at all. Then the monkey says, 'I want that attention'; then it goes to Japan to meditate, or to India to sit at someone's feet, and so on.

We are asking: is this movement of attention totally unrelated to consciousness as we know it? Obviously it is. Can this attention, as a movement, flow as all movements must flow? And when the monkey becomes active, can the monkey itself become aware that it is active and so not interfere with the flow of attention?

Somebody insulted me yesterday and the monkey was awake to reply; and because it has become aware of itself and all the implications of the monkey tricks, it subsides and lets the attention flow. Not, 'how to maintain the flow' — this is really important — the moment you say 'I must maintain it', that is the activity of the monkey. So the monkey knows when it is active and the sensitivity of its awareness immediately makes it quiet.

Questioner: In this movement of attention there is no self interest, therefore there is no resistance, no waste of energy.

KRISHNAMURTI: Sir, attention means the height of energy, doesn't it? In attention all the energy is there, not fragmented. The moment it is fragmented and action takes place, then the monkey is at work. And when the monkey, which is also learning, has become sensitive, has become aware, it realises the waste of energy and therefore, naturally, becomes quiet. It is not 'the monkey' and 'attention' — it is not a division between the monkey and attention. If there is a division the attention then becomes the 'higher self' — you know all the tricks the monkeys have invented — but attention is a total movement. It is a total action, not *opposed* to attention. Unfortunately the monkey also has its own life and wakes up.

Now, when there is no centre, when there is the complete apogee of attention, will you tell me what there is? What has happened to the mind that is so highly attentive, with not a breath of energy wasted. What takes place? Come on Sirs — I am talking all the time!

Questioner: There is total silence. There is no self-identification . . .

KRISHNAMURTI: No monkey tricks! What has happened? Not only to the intellect, to the brain, but to the body. I have talked but you don't learn! If the speaker doesn't come any more, if he dies, what is going to happen? How are you going to learn? Will you learn from some yogi? No, Sir, therefore learn *now!* What has happened to a mind that has become highly attentive, in which all the energy is there — what has happened to the quality of the intellect?

Questioner: It sees.

KRISHNAMURTI: No, you don't know! Please don't guess.

Questioner: It is totally quiet.

KRISHNAMURTI: Look, Sir — the brain which has been operating, working, which has invented the monkey — doesn't that brain become extraordinarily sensitive? If you don't know, please don't guess. And there is your body — when you have got such tremendous energy, unspoilt, unwasted, what has happened to the whole organism, to the whole structure of the human being? That is what I am asking.

Questioner: It wakes up and it becomes alive, it learns ...

KRISHNAMURTI: No. Sir, it has to become alive to learn, otherwise you can't learn. If you're asleep and say, 'I believe in my prejudice, I like my prejudice, my conditioning is marvellous' — then you're asleep, you are not awake. But the moment you question, begin to learn, you are beginning to be alive. That is not my question. What has happened to the body, to the brain?

Questioner: There is complete interaction, there is no division, but total awareness.

KRISHNAMURTI: Sir, if you are not wasting energy fiddling, what has happened to the machinery of the brain, which is purely a mechanical thing?

Questioner: It is alive.

KRISHNAMURTI: Please, sir — do watch yourself. Pay attention to something so completely, with your heart, with your body, with your mind, with everything in you, with every particle, every cell and see what takes place.

Questioner: At that time you don't exist.

KRISHNAMURTI: Yes, Sir. But what has happened to the brain, not to *you*? I agree the centre doesn't exist, but the body is there, the brain is there — what has happened to the brain?

Questioner: It rests, it regenerates.

KRISHNAMURTI: What is the function of the brain?

Questioner: Order.

KRISHNAMURTI: Don't repeat after me, for God's sake!

What is the brain? — it has evolved in time, it is the store-house of memory, it is matter, it is highly active, recognising, protecting, resisting, thinking, not thinking, frightened, seeking security and yet being uncertain, it is that brain with all its memories — not just yesterday's memories, but centuries of memories, the racial memories, the family memory, the tradition — that whole content is there. Now what has happened to that brain when there is this extraordinary attention?

Questioner: It is new . . .

KRISHNAMURTI: I don't want to be rude, but is your brain new? Or is it just a word you are saying? Please, what has happened to this brain that has become so mechanical; don't say it has become non-mechanical. The brain is purely mechanical, responding according to its conditioning, background, fears, pleasure and so on. What has happened to this mechanical brain when there is no wastage of energy at all?

Questioner: It is getting creative . . .

KRISHNAMURTI: We'll leave it till tomorrow.

8th August 1970.

Dialogue 7

Recapitulation. The mind needs order to function properly; thought mistakes security for order. The restless monkey cannot find security. The difference between stability of mind and security. The search for security only brings fragmentation. The mind that is empty of the search for security. 'No such thing as security'. To understand oneself is to understand the movement of thought. The highly attentive mind has no fragmentation of energy. Non-verbal communication. To come upon the state which is vast and timeless, in which 'the concept of death and living has quite a different meaning'.

KRISHNAMURTI: During the last five weeks that we have met here, we have been discussing and talking over together the many problems which touch our lives, the problems we create for ourselves and the society that creates them for us. We also saw that we and the society are not two different entities — they are a interrelated movement. If any person seriously concerned with and actively involved in social change — its pattern, its values, its morality — is not aware of his own conditioning, then this conditioning makes for fragmentation in action; and therefore there will be more conflict, more misery, more confusion. We went into that pretty thoroughly.

We were also discussing what fear is, and whether the mind can ever be completely and utterly free of this burden, both superficially and deeply. And we discussed the nature of pleasure, which is entirely and wholly different from joy, from delight. We also went into the question of the many fragmentations which make up our structure, our being. We saw in our discussion that these fragmentations divide and keep separate all human relationship, that one fragment assumes the authority and becomes the analyser, the censor of the other fragments.

Yesterday in talking over together the nature of consciousness we went into the question of what is attention. We said, this quality of attention is a state of mind in which all energy is highly concentrated; and in that attention there is no observer, there is no centre as the 'me' who is aware.

Now we are going to find out, learn together, what happens to the mind, to the brain, to the whole psychosomatic being, when the mind is tremendously attentive. To understand that very clearly, or find out about it for oneself, one must first see that the description is not the described. One can describe this tent, everything that is involved, but the description is not the tent. The word is not the thing, and we must be absolutely clear from the beginning that the explanation is not the explained. To be caught in description, in explanation is the most childish form of living, and I'm afraid most of us are. We are satisfied with the description, with the explanation, with saying, 'that is the cause' and just float along. Whereas what we are going to do this morning, is to find out for ourselves what has happened to the mind — the mind being the brain, as well as the whole psychosomatic structure — when there is this extraordinary attention, when there is no centre as the observer or as the censor.

To understand that, to really learn about it, not merely to be satisfied with the speaker's explanation of it, to find out, one has to begin with the understanding of 'what is'. Not what 'should be', or what 'has been', but 'what is'.

Please go with me, let's travel together, it is great fun if we move together in learning. Obviously there must be tremendous changes in the world and in ourselves. The ways of our thought and our action have become utterly immature, so contradictory, so diabolical — if one can say so. You invent a machine to kill and then there is an anti-machine to kill that machine. That's what they are doing in the world; not only socially but also mechanically. And a mind that is really concerned, involved in the seriousness of psychological as well as outward change, must go into this problem of the human being with his consciousness, with his despairs, with his appalling fears, with his ambitions, with his anxieties, with his desire to fulfil in some form or another.

So to understand all this we must begin with seeing 'what is'. 'What is' is not only what is in front of you, but what is beyond. To see what is in front of you, you must have a very clear perception, uncontaminated, not prejudiced, not involved in the desire to go beyond it, but just to observe it. Not only to observe 'what is', but what has been — which is also what is. The 'what is', *is* the past, *is* the present, and *is* the future. Do see this! So the 'what is' is not static, it is a movement. And to keep with the movement of 'what is', you need to have a very clear mind, you need to have an unprejudiced, not a distorted mind. That means, there is distortion the moment there is an effort. The mind can't see 'what is', and go beyond it, if the mind is in any way concerned with the changing of 'what is', or trying to go beyond it, or trying to suppress it.

To observe 'what is', you need energy. To observe anything attentively you need energy. To listen to what you are saying I need energy, that is, I need energy when I really, desperately want to understand what you are saying. But if I am not interested, but just listen casually, then one only needs a very slight energy that soon dissipates. So to understand 'what is' you need energy. Now, these fragmentations, of which we are, are the division of these energies. 'I' and the 'not I', 'anger' and 'not anger', 'violence' and 'not violence' — they are all fragmentations of energy. And when one fragment assumes authority over the other fragments, it is an energy that functions in fragments. Are we communicating? Communicating means learning together, working together, creating together, seeing together, understanding together; not just that I speak and you listen, and saying 'intellectually I grasp it'; that is not understanding. The whole thing is a movement in learning and therefore in action.

So the mind sees that all fragmentations, as my God, your God, my belief and your belief, are fragmentations of energy. There is only energy and fragmentation. This energy is fragmented by thought and thought is the way of conditioning —

which we won't go into again now, because we must move further.

So consciousness is the totality of these fragmentations of energy. And we said, one of those fragments is the observer, is the 'me', is the monkey who is incessantly active. Bear in mind that the description is not the described, that you are watching yourself through the words of the speaker. But the words are not the thing, therefore the speaker is of very little importance. What becomes important is your observation of yourself, of how this energy has been fragmented. Can you see that — which is 'what is' — without the fragment of the observer? Can the mind see these many fragmentations which make up the whole of consciousness? These fragments are the fragmentations of energy. Can the mind see this, without an observer who is part of the many fragments? It is important to understand this. If the mind cannot see the many fragments without looking through the eyes of another fragment, then you will never understand what attention is. Are we meeting each other?

The mind sees what fragmentation does outwardly and inwardly. Outwardly the sovereign governments, with their arms race and all the rest of it, the division of nationalities, beliefs, religious dogmas. The division in social and political action — the Labour Party, the Conservatives, the Communists, the Capitalists — is all created by the desire of thought which says, 'I must be secure'. Thought thinks it will be secure through fragmentation and so creates more fragmentation. Do you see this? Not verbally, but actually as a fact. The young and the old, the rich and the poor, death and living — do you see this constant division, this movement of fragmentation by thought, which is caught in the conditioning of these fragments? Does the mind see this whole movement without a centre that says, 'I see it'. Because the moment you have a centre, that centre becomes the factor of division. 'Me' and 'not me' — which is you. Thought has put together this 'me' through the desire, or through the impulse, to find security, safety. And in its desire to find safety

180

it has divided the energy as 'the me' and the 'not me', therefore bringing to itself insecurity. Can the mind see this as a whole? It cannot, if there is a fragment which observes.

We are asking: what is the quality of the mind that is highly attentive, in which there is no fragmentation? That is where we left off yesterday. I don't know if you have enquired, or learned from yesterday; the speaker is not a professor teaching you or giving you information. To find that out, there must be no fragmentation — obviously — which means, no effort. Effort means distortion, and as most of our minds are distorted, you cannot possibly understand what it is to be completely attentive and find out what has happened to a mind that is so utterly aware, utterly attentive.

There is a difference between security and stability. We said it is the monkey which is the everlasting 'me' with its thoughts, with its problems, with its anxieties, fears and so on. This restless thought — the monkey — is always seeking security, because it is afraid to be uncertain in its activity, in its thoughts, in its relationships. It wants everything mechanical, which is secure. So it translates security in terms of mechanical certainty. Is stability different — not opposite — but in a different dimension from security? We have to understand this. A mind that is restless and seeking security, in that restlessness it can never find stability. To be stable — firm is not the word — to be unshakeable, immovable, and yet to have the quality of great mobility! The mind that is seeking security cannot be stable in the sense of being mobile, swift, and yet immensely immovable.

Do you see the difference? Which is it you are doing in your life, in your everyday life? Is thought the monkey, seeking in its restlessness to find security, and not finding it in one direction, going off in another direction, which is the movement of restlessness? In this restlessness, it wants to find security; therefore it can never find it. It can say, 'There is God', which is still the invention of thought, the image brought about through centuries of conditioning. Or it is conditioned in the Communist world which says: 'there is no such thing', which is equally conditioning.

So what is it that you are doing — seeking security in your restlessness? The desire to be secure is one of the most curious things. And that security must be recognised by the world; I don't know whether you see this. I write a book and in the book I find my security. But that book must be recognised by the world, otherwise there is no security. So look what I've done — my security lies in the opinion of the world! 'My books sell by the thousand', and I have created the value of the world. In seeking security through a book — through whatever it is — I am depending on the world which I have created. So it means I am deceiving myself constantly. If you saw this! So the desire for thought to be secure is the way of uncertainty, is the way of insecurity. When there is complete attention in which there is no centre, what has happened to the mind that is so intensely aware? Is there security in it? Is there any sense of restlessness in it? Please don't agree — it is a tremendous thing to find this out.

You see, Sirs, most of us are seeking a solution for the misery of the world, a solution for the social morality — which is immoral. We are trying to find out a way of organising a society in which there will be no social injustice. Man has sought God, truth, whatever it is, throughout centuries, never coming upon it, but believing in it. But when you believe in it, you naturally have experiences according to your belief, which are false. So man in his restlessness, in his desire for safety, for security, to feel at ease, has invented all these imaginary securities projected by thought. When you become aware of all this fragmentation of energy — and energy is therefore no more fragmented — what has taken place in the mind that has sought security? Because it was restless, it was moving from one fear to another? Then what do you do, what is your answer?

Questioner: One is not isolated, there is no fear.

182

KRISHNAMURTI: We've been through all this, Sir. Unless it really is so with you, don't say anything, because it has no meaning. You can invent, you can say, 'I feel this' — but if you are really serious, if you want to learn about this, then you have to go into it, it is your vocation, it is your life — not just for this morning.

You know, as we were going through the village, all the people were going to church — weekend religion. This is not a weekend religion. This is a way of life, a way of living in which this energy is not broken up. If you once understood this thing, you would have an extraordinary sense of action.

Questioner: Sir, the moment you say, 'what do you do with this', the monkey within us starts up. It triggers off the question and the question triggers off the monkey.

KRISHNAMURTI: I am only putting that question to see where you are.

Questioner: Only one fragment acts.

KRISHNAMURTI: Yes. So there is one of the fragments of this broken-up energy restlessly seeking security — that is actually 'what is'. That is what we are all doing. That restlessness, and that constant search and enquiry, joining one society, then taking up another society — the monkey goes on endlessly — all that indicates a mind that is pursuing a way of life in which it is only concerned with security.

Now when that is seen very clearly, what has happened to the mind that is no longer concerned with security? Obviously it has no fear. That becomes very trivial when you see how thought has fragmented the energy, or fragmented itself, and because of this fragmentation there is fear. And when you see the activity of thought in its fragmentation, then you meet fear, you act. So we are asking, what has happened to the mind that has become extraordinarily attentive? Is there any movement of search at all? Please, find out.

Questioner: The mechanical activity stops completely.

KRISHNAMURTI: Do you understand my question? When you are so attentive, is the mind still seeking? Seeking experience, seeking to understand itself, seeking to go beyond itself, seeking to find out right action, wrong action, seeking a permanency on which it can depend — permanency in relationship, or in belief, or in some conclusion? Is that still going on, when you are so completely aware?

Questioner: The mind does not seek anything any longer.

KRISHNAMURTI: Do you know what that means, when you make a statement of that kind so easily? Not to seek anything — which means what?

Questioner: It is already to receive something new that it cannot imagine.

KRISHNAMURTI: No, madam, you really have not understood. My question is, the mind has seen the activity of the monkey in its restlessness. This activity — which is still energy — thought has broken up in its desire to find a permanent security, a certainty, safety. And so it has divided the world as the 'me' and the 'not me', 'we' and 'they', and is seeking truth as a way of security. When one has observed all this, is the mind seeking anything at all any more? Seeking implies restlessness — I haven't found security here, and I go there, and I haven't found it there so I go elsewhere.

Questioner: The mind then is not concerned with search.

KRISHNAMURTI: A mind which is without a centre is not concerned with search. But is it taking place with you?

Questioner: At the moment you are attentive it is taking place.

...NAMURTI: No, Sir.

Questioner: All sorts of things happen to the mind when it stops striving.

KRISHNAMURTI: Have you ever known, walking or sitting quietly, what it means to be completely empty? Not isolated, not withdrawn, not building a wall around yourself and finding you have no relationship with anything — I don't mean that. When the mind is completely empty, it does not mean that it has no memory, the memories are there, because you are walking to your house, or are going to your office. But I mean the emptiness of a mind that has finished with all the movement of search.

Questioner: All is and I am. What is 'I am'? Who is 'I am'? Who is this 'I' that says 'am'? The monkey?

KRISHNAMURTI: Don't repeat what the propagandists have said, what the religions have said, what the psychologists have said. Who says, 'I am'? — the Italian, the Frenchman, the Russian, the believer, the dogma, the fears, the past, the seeker, and the one who seeks and finds? Or the one who is identified with the house, with the husband, with the money, with the name, with the family — which are all words! No, you don't see this. But it is so! If you see that you are a bundle of memories and words, the restless monkey comes to an end.

Questioner: If your mind is completely empty when you are walking to the office, why are you walking to the office? Why are you still doing this?

KRISHNAMURTI: You have to earn a livelihood, you have to go to your home, you will be going out of this tent.

Questioner: Surely the question is, how can I be empty if memory is operating.

KRISHNAMURTI: Now look, Sir, I want to tell you a very ___
thing: there is no such thing as security. This restless demand for
security is the part of the observer, the centre, the monkey. And
this restless monkey — which is thought — has broken up this
world and has made a frightful mess of it, it has brought such
misery, such agony! And thought cannot solve this, however intelligent, however clever, erudite, capable of efficient thinking,
thought cannot possibly bring order out of this chaos. There
must be a way out of it which is not thought. I want to
convey to you that in that state of attention, in that movement
of attention, all sense of security has gone, because there is
stability. That stability has nothing whatsoever to do with security — when thought seeks security it makes it into something
permanent, immovable, and therefore it becomes mechanical.
Thought seeks security in relationship. In that relationship
thought creates an image. That image becomes the permanent
and breaks up the relationship — you have your image and I
have mine. In that image thought has established and identified
itself as the permanent thing.

Outwardly this is what we have done: your country, my
country, and so on. When the mind has left all that, left it in the
sense that it has seen the utter futility, the mischief of it, it has
finished with it. Then what takes place in the mind which has
completely finished with the whole concept of security? What
happens to that mind which is so attentive that it is completely
stable, so that thought is no longer seeking security in any form
and sees that there is no such thing as the permanent? I'm
pointing it out to you; the description is not the described.

See the importance of this; the brain has evolved with the
idea of being completely secure. The mind, the brain wants
security, otherwise it can't function. Without order it will
function illogically, neurotically, inefficiently, therefore the
brain is always wanting order and it has translated having order
in terms of security. If that brain is still functioning, it is still

seeking order through security. So when there is attention, is the brain still seeking security?

Questioner: Sir, there is only the present.

KRISHNAMURTI: Sir, I am trying to convey something to you. I may be totally wrong. I may be talking complete nonsense, but you have to find out for yourself if I am talking nonsense.

Questioner: I get the sensation that at the moment I am attentive, I am not seeking. But that attention may cease; then I am seeking again.

KRISHNAMURTI: *Never!* That's the whole point. If thought sees that there is no such thing as permanency, thought will *never* seek it again. That is, the brain, with its memories of security, its cultivation in a society depending on security, with all its ideas and its morality based on security, that brain has become completely empty of all movements towards security.

Have you ever gone into this question of meditation, any of you? Meditation is not concerned with meditation but with the meditator — do you see the difference? Most of you are concerned with meditation, what to do about it, how to meditate step by step and so on — that is not the question at all. The meditator is the meditation. To understand the meditator is meditation.

Now if you have gone into this question of meditation, the meditator must come to an end, by understanding, not by suppressing, not by killing thought. That is, to understand oneself is to understand the movement of thought; thought being the movement of the brain with all its memories — the movement of thought seeking security, and all the rest of it.

Now the meditator is asking, can this brain become completely quiet? Which is, can thought be completely still, and yet operate out of this stillness not as an end in itself. Probably all this is too complicated for you — it's really quite simple.

So the mind that is highly attentive has no fragmentation of energy. Please see that; there is no fragmentation of energy, it is *complete* energy. And that energy operates without fragmentation when you go to the office.

Questioner: Maybe a real understanding could be arrived at without the help of the word; it's a kind of direct contact with the thing you are trying to understand. And consequently there is no need for words, which are an escape.

KRISHNAMURTI: That's it. Can you communicate without words? Because words hinder.

Questioner: Yes.

KRISHNAMURTI: Look, Sir, can I communicate with you without words about the quality of the mind that is so extraordinarily attentive, and yet functions in the world without breaking the energy into fragments? You've understood my question?

Questioner: Yes.

KRISHNAMURTI: Now, can I communicate that to you without the word? How do you know I can? What are you all talking about!

Questioner: I think you can.

KRISHNAMURTI: Look, one has talked for nearly five weeks, explained everything, gone into it in detail, poured one's heart into it. Have you understood it — verbally even? And you want to understand something non-verbally! It can be done if your mind is in contact with the speaker with the same intensity, with the same passion, at the same time, at the same level, then you will communicate. Are you? Now listen to that train!

Without the word communication has been established, because we are both of us listening to the rattle of that train, at the same moment, with the same intensity, with the same passion. Only then is there direct communion. Are you intense about this at the same time as the speaker? Of course not. Sir, when you hold the hand of another, you can hold it out of habit or custom. Or you can hold it and communication can take place without a word, because both are at the given moment intense. But we are not intense, not passionate and concerned.

Questioner: Not all the time.

KRISHNAMURTI: Don't say that, not even for a minute!

Questioner: How do you know?

KRISHNAMURTI: I don't know. If you are, then you will know what it means to be aware, to be attentive, and therefore no longer seeking security; therefore you are no longer acting or thinking in terms of fragmentation. Look what has happened to a mind that has gone through all the things which we have been talking about, all the discussions and exchange of words. What has happened to the mind that has really listened to this?

First of all, it has become sensitive, not only mentally but physically. It has given up smoking, drinking, drugs. And when we have talked over this question of attention, you'll see that the mind is no longer seeking anything at all, or asserting anything. And such a mind is completely mobile and yet wholly stable. Out of that stability and sensitivity it can act without breaking life or energy up into fragments. What does such a mind find, apart from action, apart from stability? Man has always sought what he considered to be God, truth; he has always striven after it out of fear, out of his hopelessness, out of his despair and disorder. He sought it and he thought he found it. And the discovery of that he began to organise.

So that which is stable, highly mobile, sensitive, is not seeking; it sees something which has never been found, which means, time for such a mind does not exist at all — which does not mean one is going to miss a train. So there is a state which is timeless and therefore incredibly vast.

This is something most marvellous if you come upon it. I can go into it, but the description is not the described. It's for you to learn all this by looking at yourself — no book, no teacher can teach you about this — don't depend on anyone, don't join spiritual organisations, one has to learn all this out of oneself. And there the mind will discover things that are incredible. But for that, there must be no fragmentation and therefore immense stability, swiftness, mobility. To such a mind there is no time and therefore this whole concept of death and living has quite a different meaning.

9th August 1970.